From
Conflict
—— to ——
Courage

From
Conflict
—— to ——
Courage

How to Stop
Avoiding and
Start Leading

MARLENE CHISM

Berrett–Koehler Publishers, Inc.

Berrett-Koehler Publishers, Inc.
1333 Broadway, Suite 1000
Oakland, CA 94612-1921
Tel: (510) 817-2277
Fax: (510) 817-2278
www.bkconnection.com

ORDERING INFORMATION
Quantity sales. Special discounts are available on quantity purchases by corporations, associations, and others. For details, contact the "Special Sales Department" at the Berrett-Koehler address above.
Individual sales. Berrett-Koehler publications are available through most bookstores. They can also be ordered directly from Berrett-Koehler: Tel: (800) 929-2929; Fax: (802) 864-7626; www.bkconnection.com.
Orders for college textbook / course adoption use. Please contact Berrett-Koehler: Tel: (800) 929-2929; Fax: (802) 864-7626.

Distributed to the U.S. trade and internationally by Penguin Random House Publisher Services.

Berrett-Koehler and the BK logo are registered trademarks of Berrett-Koehler Publishers, Inc.

Printed in Canada

Berrett-Koehler books are printed on long-lasting acid-free paper. When it is available, we choose paper that has been manufactured by environmentally responsible processes. These may include using trees grown in sustainable forests, incorporating recycled paper, minimizing chlorine in bleaching, or recycling the energy produced at the paper mill.

Library of Congress Cataloging-in-Publication Data
Names: Chism, Marlene, author.
Title: From conflict to courage : how to stop avoiding and start leading / Marlene Chism.
Description: First Edition. | Oakland, CA : Berrett-Koehler Publishers, 2022. | Includes bibliographical references and index.
Identifiers: LCCN 2021050938 (print) | LCCN 2021050939 (ebook) | ISBN 9781523000722 (paperback) | ISBN 9781523000739 (pdf) | ISBN 9781523000746 (epub)
Subjects: LCSH: Conflict management. | Communication in management. | Leadership.
Classification: LCC HD42 .C45 2022 (print) | LCC HD42 (ebook) | DDC 658.4/053—dc23/eng/20211210
LC record available at https://lccn.loc.gov/2021050938
LC ebook record available at https://lccn.loc.gov/2021050939

First Edition
28 27 26 25 24 23 22   10 9 8 7 6 5 4 3 2 1

Book producer: Happenstance Type-O-Rama
Text designer: Maureen Forys, Happenstance Type-O-Rama
Cover designer: Adam Johnson
Author photo: Kristy Perryman Photography

→ For my first teachers: ←
Mom and Dad

Contents

Preface

I used to think conflict was due to some difficult personality or situation, but then one day I started playing with an idea: the idea that there is no conflict unless there's an inner conflict. When you're disturbed, angry, emotional, or impatient, when you're thinking about what other people are doing wrong, or when you're dredging up the past and rehashing old grudges, you'll have conflict even when no one else is physically in the room. I asked myself the question, Could it be that the first step to effectively managing conflict is to resolve inner conflict first? To be sure, you can't resolve inner conflict if you don't even know you have it, so I started paying attention to how inner conflict arises and grows in my own life. I'm willing to share my challenges for the purpose of learning.

Inner conflict arises when I want something but I hesitate to ask for what I want, or when I'm impatient but everything around me is moving slowly. Inner conflict grows when I believe every thought without challenging my narrative, or when I assume I know someone's motives but don't have the courage to question their behaviors. Inner conflict deepens when I hold a grudge or continue to harbor past resentments. When I put off a conversation because I fear the other person's defensiveness, it's only my inner conflict keeping me from moving forward; after all, the conversation hasn't even happened yet.

One of the most difficult aspects of leadership is managing conflict instead of avoiding it. My hope is that after reading this book, you will no longer avoid conflict but instead realize that conflict can be your greatest teacher and a catalyst for leadership growth.

Conflict Is Not the Problem

Leaders have an opportunity to be a channel for chaos or a catalyst for clarity.

One of the toughest parts of your job as a leader is managing conflict. You'll have to initiate difficult conversations about performance with employees you care for, and you'll have to speak about behavioral issues with those you wish would move on. The conflicts you'll face on your leadership journey won't only be with employees. Having a title or positional power doesn't make conflict any easier; advancement requires you to become more conflict capable. You'll experience conflict with those in higher power, perhaps a board of directors, a top-level executive, a peer, a partner, a vendor, or a client. You'll have to make difficult decisions where you feel misaligned and uncertain, and you'll feel "inner conflict," that feeling when your values clash. Conflict can be seen as a problem that keeps you stuck, or conflict can be seen as a teacher that helps you grow.

———————— Why I Wrote This Book ————————

I wrote this book because the ideas in this book have helped me and thousands of other leaders, and I think the ideas, tips, techniques, and methods will help you. My philosophy is this: if I've had a problem, it means I'm not alone. It means millions of other people have the same problem or will have the same problem. Everything I now teach, speak, or write about is something I either have worked through or am working on.

I'm not trying to be a guru. It's dangerous to put anyone on a pedestal or give someone else the responsibility for your decisions. I don't believe in gurus, but I believe in teachers. Teachers show up as authors, speakers, facilitators, thought leaders, professors, or experts.

Our teachers also show up as the boss we can't stand, the complaining coworker who drains our energy, the employee that won't engage, and the person who has a different political viewpoint. *Teachers are all around us if we have the eyes to see.* I'm inviting you, as you read through this book, to see conflict as your teacher and me as the facilitator.

Over the last twenty years of working with other leaders, I observed that conflict that had escalated to creating a toxic work environment was due to one simple area of neglect: a conversation that should have happened but didn't. I saw avoidance of conflict at every level in almost every organization.

I've also surveyed hundreds of leaders in various industries over the years to get a sense of how they viewed conflict and how they assessed their own skills and confidence around resolving conflict. The more experienced the leader, the more awareness they seemed to have about their conflict aversion and lack of capabilities. The more experienced leaders scored themselves as average in confidence and competence, indicating they knew there was room to grow. What was interesting was how new or inexperienced leaders perceived their competencies. The least experienced leaders scored high on both confidence and capabilities. For example, new supervisors in manufacturing, construction, healthcare, or education often overestimated their ability to manage conflict. Instead of avoiding, they were overly aggressive; I would say a little "drunk with power." Others used appeasing as a way to get everyone to like them. All leaders had the desire to be good leaders, but they often lacked specific skills to have conversations in a way that inspired or motivated employees. When the issues included conflict with their superiors, appeasing seemed to be the top coping method. While many leaders gave head nods and lip service to embracing conflict, very few of them lived that reality in their leadership behavior. In private conversations, top leaders admit that they want to avoid or eliminate conflict.

What This Book Is About

This book isn't about avoiding or eliminating conflict. It's about redefining conflict. This book isn't as much about embracing conflict as it is about facing conflict. This book isn't about getting agreement from others; it's about seeking alignment within. This book isn't about changing others, or changing the world; it's about transforming yourself.

The paradox is that when you see conflict as a teacher, when you define conflict differently, courageously face conflict, and work on transforming yourself first, you often get the agreement or the resolution you were seeking. You change minds. People open up. They grow. You get collaboration and not just compliance. Instead of trying to change others, you become the change.

Who This Book Is For

This book is for anyone who identifies as being a leader, regardless of your level of power, political orientation, gender, race, religion, seniority, industry, or education. This book is for any leader who says, "I have an anger problem, and I'm embarrassed that I don't know how to control my triggers." This book is for the leader who is thinking about leaving because they don't know what to do next or where to start, the leader who wishes everyone could just get along but it just gets worse. This book is for the leader who doesn't know how to ask for support. This book is for any leader who has a hard-to-get-along-with boss or colleague that undermines their leadership or employees who make the open door a revolving door full of complaints. This is for any leader who wishes their employees felt more empowered. This book is for any leader who has already had all the training offered by their own corporation, as well as the leader who works for a small organization with no resources to devote to leadership development. This book is for leaders who want to create a book club and are courageous enough to learn from someone in a "lower" position and not intimidated to learn from someone more senior. This book is for any leader who wishes they'd had that conversation sooner and now they don't know where to start. This book is for an employee who wants to be a leader but doesn't have experience or confidence. This book is for anyone who thinks conflict is a problem.

———— Why Conflict Is Not the Problem ————

Most leaders avoid conflict because they see conflict as a problem, *but conflict isn't really the problem; mismanagement is.* How do leaders mismanage conflict? By avoiding it, putting it on the back burner, getting emotional when they need to stay calm, or getting aggressive when they're at capacity. Leaders mismanage conflict when they keep important issues from their boss because they don't want to be seen as incompetent. Leaders mismanage conflict when fear guides their behaviors—for example, when they don't listen to employees who feel misunderstood or mistreated or who experience gender, religious, or racial discrimination.

When employees complain about each other, mismanagement includes moving people around to different departments to appease someone or listening privately to hearsay to get a leg up on what's happening. These methods almost always backfire. Even if the mismanagement is unintentional, by not facing the issues head on, leaders increase misunderstandings and risk to the organization.

Leaders mismanage conflict when they promote the "pot stirrer" to another position, give special favors to someone they feel sorry for, or forget to document their progress. There are dozens of ways we leaders mismanage conflict, and we'll talk more in depth about those ways later, but let's first look at the cost of mismanaging conflict.

——————— The Cost to the Organization ———————

It's estimated that employees spend almost three hours per week arguing, and those arguments amount to $359 billion in hours that are focused on conflict instead of on productivity.[1] That's a big cost to time and productivity. Now think about what happens when these small arguments go on for too long and blow up because the manager doesn't know about the conflicts or doesn't know what to do, or when the manager does try to intervene and the conflict is mismanaged. I've seen numerous examples where a complaint was ignored, employees were shuffled to different departments, and after a year or two, the problem turned into a harassment or discrimination complaint.

The US Equal Employment Opportunity Commission (EEOC) had 67,448 charges of workplace discrimination in fiscal year 2020, with *retaliation* cited as the largest percentage of all charges filed. Although the trend is moving downward, with 5,227 fewer cases than in 2019, the results show that there's still a lot of work to do and a lot to learn. The fact remains that unresolved conflict is costly. The agency secured $439.2 million for victims of discrimination in the private sector and state and local government workplaces through voluntary resolutions and litigation.[2]

To quote the EEOC release at eeoc.gov: "The agency responded to over 470,000 calls to its toll-free number and more than 187,000 inquiries in field offices, including 122,775 inquiries through the online intake and appointment scheduling system, reflecting the significant public demand for EEOC's services."

An employment discrimination case can take two to three years to reach a reasonable resolution and thousands if not hundreds of thousands of dollars in legal fees.[3] Financial costs notwithstanding, any leader or employee who has gone through an investigation knows how distracting the mental and emotional toll can be on collaboration and productivity.

The Cost to Well-Being

Conflict doesn't feel good. Leaders are human beings, and we humans tend to avoid situations and people that make us think things we don't want to think and feel things we don't like to feel. When you're preoccupied with conflict, it affects your sleep, your nervous system, and your ability to make rational decisions. In simple terms, these experiences create a thought-feeling loop.

Let's look at the thought-feeling loop that happens when we're immersed in a very small conflict. Suppose your employees are coming in late, and they're gathering at the coffee shop before work hours, and they've missed meetings and important phone calls. You think to yourself: "They all know better! I've addressed this issue twice, and I'm being ignored." Now you feel resentment. You don't like the choices you're faced with, but you also realize you've let your employees get by with the behavior. You enjoyed the fact that they have camaraderie, but now it's affecting productivity. The behavior allowed has become the standard. The last time you had a performance conversation with the supervisor of this team, you got resistance and excuses. You got roped into a nonproductive conversation playing ping-pong: yes, I did; no, you didn't; that's not fair; and I knew you would say that, and here's what everyone else thinks. You took the bait and engaged in nonproductive hearsay. Then there was the time one of the employees cried when you tried to intervene. You feel stuck and angry. How can they do this to you when you're so nice to them? Don't they realize what you're up against?

This example is a small but common conflict compared to a conflict that has escalated, but the point is that unmanaged conflict affects your productivity and well-being simply because you're a human being, and human beings have a brain and emotions. It helps to know how it all works.

I'm not a neuroscientist or a psychologist. My goal isn't to overwhelm you with information you won't remember. My goal is to provide ideas you can remember and use—something practical for your leadership growth. So here it is. An emotional experience is triggered in the body, and that leads to an interpretation or a series of thoughts. The thoughts lead to feelings such as fear, resentment, anger, rejection, and sadness, to name a few. These feelings lead to thoughts about revenge, retaliation, and retreat, which produce chemicals in the brain that motivate you to do whatever it takes to make it all stop. This cycle is what is responsible for bad decisions such as avoiding, appeasing, aggression, or what I call "moving the chess pieces around," shuffling employees to different departments to keep peace. When the employee who was moved perceives your action as unfair, or as retaliation, you've just created a much bigger problem than the one you were trying to avoid.

But you're not at the mercy of your thoughts and feelings. With a little work, you can develop a measure of control over your thoughts, feelings, interpretations, and behaviors. The bottom line is that when you mismanage conflict, you feel it. Mismanaged conflict affects your well-being. Mismanaged conflict also affects your leadership growth.

The Cost to Growth

When you avoid a difficult conversation, you wire your brain to avoid. While you might breathe a sigh of relief initially, this pattern of avoidance becomes your go-to method for anything that triggers you. Just as avoidance hampers growth, so does the pattern of aggression. Aggression is a sign that you don't have the right tools for managing stress when the heat is on. Aggressive behavior makes a statement about who's in charge and can create compliance, but it rarely contributes to collaboration, connection, or creativity.

The Cost to Collaboration

When there's serious conflict, the missing pieces are often related to trust, relationships, and collaboration. When the proper foundation of trust is laid, conflict is relatively easy to manage and resolve, but without trust, small conflicts erode collaboration.

For over twenty years I worked in manufacturing. I wasn't in Human Resources, and I wasn't a manager. I worked on the lines. I did everything from packing product to stacking skids to driving a fork-lift to tearing down equipment for sanitation on third shift. I had many great bosses who helped me to grow, but I also had some bosses who were my "teachers" and who mismanaged conflict. At one point in time, I had an overly aggressive (and avoidant) boss. If anyone had a complaint, he would say, "That's just the way it is. I didn't ask you to work here. If you don't like it, find another place to work." There were times when employees had ideas to improve production, stop a jam on the production lines, or prevent tendonitis, but he didn't want to hear it. His aggressive behavior made him seem unapproachable. When you mismanage conflict by resorting to aggression, people don't want to approach you and you don't get their best work, their ideas, or their engagement. You get resistance at worst and compliance at best. If there's excessive turnover in one department, look at two things: the job itself and the department leader.

A Message to Leaders

My advice to aspiring leaders is this: before you say yes to becoming a leader, understand your culture, understand the dynamics of conflict, get familiar with your own reactions to conflict, and learn how to manage yourself before trying to resolve conflict with others. Know this: even though the organization may not have the resources to offer mentoring, coaching, or skills development, you must take the initiative to learn anyway because if conflict escalates to the point of getting attorneys involved, the easiest path to end the drama is to fire you. That's the uncomfortable reality in many organizations.

The good news is there's something practical you can do if you're a frontline leader. Ask for mentoring. See if you can get your boss to agree to speak with you on a *scheduled basis* to discuss your decision-making. Be humble and make the case that you're looking out for the good of the organization. This is easy if you admire your boss and more difficult if you don't. The very fact that you asked will elevate your boss's awareness and will help you form a better relationship and understand things from their viewpoint. If your boss is growth oriented, they will be happy you asked. This keeps the door open when you start to have problems. These days, transparency is not really a choice; it's a given. You'll either choose transparency up front or be exposed later. When you let your boss know what you're up to, you'll never be accused of hiding information.

For more seasoned leaders, my advice is this: know how to identify red flags that conflict is brewing. Become aware of small complaints, resentments, blame, noncompliance, and other negative vibes that indicate something's wrong. Don't brush off complaints and negativity as someone's character flaw. Instead, interpret these behaviors as a sign that a conversation needs to happen. Learn how to initiate inquisitive conversations to uncover what's really going on. If you see yourself as a "hands off" leader, my suggestion is to become a bit more hands on so that you aren't caught off guard when things blow up. The biggest concern is "I don't want to micromanage." There's a wide gap between having a light touch, having a hands-on approach, and micromanaging. It's your responsibility to know how things are being managed when you're in charge. This requires you to get honest about the way *you* handle conflict because, ultimately, you're a role model in the organization. If you admit that you aren't that confident or competent when it comes to conflict, that's perfectly OK. Don't judge yourself. The truth will set you free! You can grab some skills and understanding now and make learning your own choice, or you will be forced to learn later. And when learning is forced, you'll spend hours consuming content that may not help you the way you need to be helped.

We live in a litigious society, and my belief is that we could significantly reduce workplace lawsuits if we knew how to build trust and create a culture of inclusion, curiosity, and camaraderie. Mismanaging conflict creates lack of clarity, and where there's lack of clarity, there are negative experiences, and when people feel discounted, retaliated against, or excluded, there will be division and misunderstandings that waste time and take years to repair, if ever. The conversation avoided today is the lawsuit three years later.

I'm not suggesting that the reason to get better at conflict is to avoid lawsuits or work the system. My message is that if the system needs to be changed, we are the system. The change starts with me. The change starts with you—how you think, how you behave, and how you courageously address and manage conflict. As leaders, we need to stop looking for all of the answers on the outside of ourselves and, instead, become the change we seek to end sexism, prejudice, injustice, and inequality. The part we can most easily control and change is ourselves. It benefits us personally to nurture relationships so that work is both enjoyable and productive. In addition, it makes business sense to be able to identify and manage conflict before it gets out of hand.

Here's the unfortunate reality: once your organization perceives they are at risk due to leadership mismanagement, it'll become mandatory to watch hours of sensitivity training or other video presentations, not necessarily for the purpose of leadership growth, or because it's a good idea, but instead for the purpose of *proving* that the organization cares and that they take the problems seriously. Even though there's some good training out there, it might not help you build better relationships and give you exercises to become better at self-regulation. The standard trainings might give you insights but not help you to learn why people do what they do, and this type of training most likely won't give you a blueprint for initiating difficult conversations.

This book will.

The Opportunity for All Leaders

We are living in exciting yet volatile times. There are many global issues affecting us all, and let's face it, many of us are uncomfortable engaging in conversations about important issues of gender equality, political division, social justice, racial tensions, and human rights. As I write this, we are in the second wave of experiencing COVID-19, a devastating pandemic affecting the entire globe. We should know by now that what affects one of us affects us all. Instead, we see division, conversations about conspiracy, political agendas, and fear about other people's intentions. What does this have to do with the workplace? These issues are so profound and expansive, and our access to connectivity through the internet is allowing unchecked controversy that's now leaking into every crack and crevice of the workplace. People are divided, and they don't know how to disentangle from the heat of conflict. Leaders have an opportunity to be a force for division or a force for unity, a channel for confusion or a catalyst for clarity.

Social Media: A Snapshot of Conflict to Come

Amid the pandemic, I saw a post from a social media influencer and business entrepreneur, a seven-figure businesswoman with a massive following. The context on her social media thread was clearly about COVID-19, but many, including me, thought the message was unclear. Others thought they knew exactly what she intended.

This entrepreneurial thought leader posted a beautiful picture of herself with a concerned look on her face, and the copy said, "Me hoping more humans 'wake up' soon, otherwise this perma-fear clown town will never end, and our children's future freedoms will never be the same."

The themes were about freedom, fear, the pandemic, and wishing more people would awaken, but what was she asking people to awaken to? Was she asking for more people to be vaccinated, or was her message to awaken to an idea that a pandemic is nothing to fear so we should go about business as usual? Was she for masking or against masking? Was she talking conspiracy theory or science? Curious, I scrolled down and read a couple dozen of the more than six hundred comments and over seventy shares. Here's a sampling in no particular order, but all of these particular comments were speaking directly to the thought leader:

"I 100 percent agree!"

"Love seeing more leaders like this speak up!"

"Why don't you share a real point of view instead of talking in code to your tribe. I don't know what this post is about."

"You are entitled and privileged. You need to wake up!"

"It's much worse for China and other countries!"

"You're not awake you're paranoid."

"What planet did you come from?"

"What is your post about? I don't know what you mean?"

"It's no longer our job to wake up the sheep, it's time to wake up other lions!"

"None of us knows what this really means and look at how we're giving it all this energy!"

Did this thought leader intentionally post something controversial to get engagement? My perception is that this business leader usually sends a unifying message that is very inclusive of all viewpoints. At the same time, with thousands of followers, she's also a savvy businesswoman, and she knows how to increase algorithms. High engagement mixed with high controversy means you're cutting through the noise.

———— The "Us versus Them" Mentality ————

I didn't feel good after reading this post. I felt concerned about the ways in which we're all handling conflict. "But wait a minute, this is social media," you say. "These verbal attacks only happen where people can hide behind their computer screens or devices." Many downplay the insensitivities and incivility on social media because it's "virtual," and many think this kind of behavior won't happen in real life, face to face. My belief is that we're becoming desensitized to disruptive behavior on social media, and this type of "entertainment" and exposure is building a platform for more intense and unpredictable conflict. When I see name-calling, judgment, accusations, and misunderstandings based only on a partial understanding of the issue at hand, I wonder if this is a forewarning of what's to come in face-to-face conversations in the workplace, at the grocery store, in airports, and beyond.

While reading through the thread, I realized I was getting distracted. It drew me in—not enough to get entangled in conflict, but enough to observe some of the common themes I'm addressing in this book: conflict capacity, leadership identity, leadership clarity, emotional integrity, structures, and choice. I'd like to expand on these themes right now and how these themes are showing up in our workplaces and in our world.

Many of the participants on this conversation thread showed a complete lack of conflict capacity: being offended without taking a pause to understand or question intentions, relying only on one's own interpretation, and when at capacity, resorting to name-calling, judgment, and accusations—divisive language about who is awakened and who is not, conversations about "who are the sheep" and "who are the lions." The tone of superiority and disrespect was palpable; I could feel it in my bones.

This behavior is not just about social media. The heart of the issue is "us versus them." The us versus them mentality is alive and well in the workplace as much as it is on social media. The reality is, we have a choice to ignore social media. We can shut down our devices and ignore what's right in front of us, or we can observe the trends. Today's leader needs more than skill sets to deal with high-conflict situations that escalate without much warning. Let me give you an overview of what to expect in this book.

An Overview

In **chapter 1**, we'll talk about why skill building is important but insufficient on its own and why the inner game is necessary for good decision-making in today's time. Today's leader needs conflict capacity, the result of which expands a leader's courage to listen when it's difficult, get curious when they're certain, and practice critical thinking when it's easier to follow the crowd.

In **chapter 2**, we explore how identity drives behavior. On social media it's pretty easy to see what someone identifies with most, whether it's gender, race, politics, women's rights, religion, health-care, country, or any combination of identities. I'd venture to say that what we identify with the most creates the most vulnerability when that identity is questioned or threatened. Observe conflicts on public forums and you'll notice that very few people are curious about opposing views. (The truth is, very few of us are willing to consider another point of view when we feel threatened, discounted, or violated.) That's why it's important for leaders to understand how to spot distractions and gain leadership clarity instead of resorting to appeasing or aggression when difficulties arise, and to model civility and curiosity.

Chapter 3 presents a method to help leaders gain leadership clarity. How can a leader make good decisions when they can't describe the current situation, can't articulate the intended outcome, and don't understand the perceived or real obstacles? You can't change a situation if you don't understand it, and you can't help someone get what they want if you don't understand them. Without clarity there is no alignment. Leadership clarity helps leaders make aligned business decisions.

My goal with **chapter 4** is to do some myth-busting around anger. It's common for clients to confess to me that they have an anger problem. If you struggle to self-regulate, or if you work with a hothead, this chapter sheds some light. You'll see that anger has its place and that managed emotions produce decisive, purposeful action versus destructive, self-serving action.

In **chapter 5**, we'll look at conflict from a different lens, to realize that not every issue is about personality: sometimes the conflict is due in part to the visible and invisible structures that invite conflict. We'll explore the ways in which leaders can shape structures (invisible and visible) to determine the behaviors they want to see.

In **chapter 6**, we get to the heart of dealing with negativity, game playing, excuses, blaming, and other dysfunctional behaviors that hamper productivity and waste time. You'll learn how to quickly identify pockets of resistance. For anyone working with a difficult colleague, a complainer who doesn't want your advice, or a closed-minded coworker, this chapter offers strength training you can use in multiple areas of life.

If you need to initiate a difficult conversation but don't have the skills or don't know where to start, **chapter 7** offers a complete blueprint of where to start, how to think about the conversation, and how to promote accountability. You'll learn how to use intention to guide the conversation so that you aren't talking just to "document" but to inspire and support the employee to improve performance.

Chapter 8 is about the greatest power we all have, the power of choice. One of my aspirations is to help people become the creative force in their own lives. As long as we buy into a victim narrative, we imprison ourselves. Leaders have a new choice to make, the choice to see the value in each human being and to help them realize their own power through their choices. Many of our daily conflicts would end if we could recognize the power of choice.

Conflict mismanagement is a problem, but there's a big opportunity for leaders to become change agents. As a leader, you aren't going to solve world problems or make people change their habits on social media, and you probably won't convince someone to see politics, religion, or world events differently if they aren't open to conversation. What you can do is model the behavior of one who knows how to manage conflict so that you can build trust, collaboration, and inclusion—a real sense of purpose and belonging—so that mismanaged conflict doesn't escalate in your own workplace.

1

Conflict Capacity: Comfort Is Not a Requirement

Skills development that doesn't lead to embodiment is just a notch above entertainment.

My tolerance for certain types of personalities was limited when I first started working for myself. I found it difficult to be around know-it-all aggressive types—those who are extremely resistant and argumentative. When they became confrontational, I either avoided or became passive-aggressive. I didn't mean to, but I couldn't seem to help myself. Once I got triggered, my sarcasm, quick wit, or eye-rolling seemed to manifest out of thin air. This was a vicious emotional cycle of anger, regret, and aggression. I didn't want negative people to bring me down. My justifications seemed reasonable. I'd say, "Business doesn't have to be this difficult" and "It's for my own peace of mind."

I studied the effects of negativity, and I justified eliminating negative people from my life. But something kept eating at me. I believed in personal responsibility. I believed we're all responsible for our experience. I believed Eleanor Roosevelt—"No one can make you feel anything without your agreement"—and all the other motivational quotes you hear on TED talks and Instagram. And even though I believed in personal responsibility, secretly I blamed *them* (negative people, complainers, high-conflict individuals) for being who they were. My real conflict was internal: my divided mind. To be honest, I wanted *them* to change. I didn't want to change myself. If she could just accept things instead of complaining. If he would listen better. If he wasn't so rude. If they were a little more self-aware.

There are a lot of misunderstandings when it comes to managing conflict and keeping peace. When we say, "I don't tolerate drama" and "I keep negative people completely out of my life," we are in essence saying that by controlling outer circumstances and avoiding certain types of people, everything will be fine. I'm now convinced that these beliefs are an incomplete way of understanding conflict and our ability to expand enough to truly manage and resolve conflict. To manage conflict effectively, we need to redefine conflict, recognize our dysfunctional patterns, and then work on expanding our conflict capacity. Let's get started.

———— The First Way We Mismanage Conflict ————

The first way we mismanage conflict is how we view and define conflict. We make conflict personal; then our brains look for evidence to support our views. Most of us view conflict as some version of win-lose, right versus wrong, us versus them, liberal versus conservative. Sound familiar? All you have to do is go to social media during an election year and you'll be reminded of how mismanaged conflict can escalate and contribute to personal loss. The dictionary definitions won't encourage you either: A state of open prolonged fighting. A fight or a disagreement. A state of disagreement or disharmony between persons or ideas; a clash. A battle or war.[1] No wonder most of us have such an aversion to conflict.

What definition of conflict would be more helpful for building conflict capacity? What if you defined conflict in such a way that you no longer had to worry about who's to blame or think of the other as an enemy? What if you could view conflict in such a way as to be able to initiate difficult conversations that get results? Would that be more valuable to you? You bet it would. Redefining conflict in a way that took all the emotional and mental pain away would help you to build conflict capacity so that, as a result, you would be a better leader, a better partner, and a better friend.

Let me share a mental model that has significantly helped me, and I hope it helps you too. My definition of conflict is to view conflict as *misalignment due to opposing drives, desires, and demands.* This definition takes personality out of the equation, eliminates your assumptions about motive, and makes conflict much more interesting. Think of two arrows going in opposite directions (see figure 1).

The arrows represent the opposing drives, desires, and demands between two people or—surprise—even within yourself, with no one around to argue at all. Should I, or shouldn't I? If I do this, then I might miss out on that. I'm not sure. Yes, I've decided . . . no, I haven't. If you've ever stayed on the hamster wheel of indecision, you understand the cost to your mental health of not having clarity and alignment. The point here is that conflict is a misalignment that happens because there are opposing drives, desires, and demands.

When two business unit managers argue over budget, it's not because they're bad people; it's because they haven't found ways

Conflict

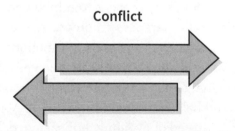

Opposing drives, desires, and demands

FIGURE 1. Conflict

to align their opposing desires, drives, and demands, and they can't align until they have a conversation and seek to understand. Nor can they collaborate or compromise when all the elements within the conflict are yet to be uncovered. It's not necessarily conflicts that ruin relationships. It's the emotions and behaviors that emerge from a response to mismanaged conflict: *disrespect, discounting, and dismissing.* Think about the conflicts you've had. Did you give the other person the benefit of the doubt? Did you get curious as to why they saw things the way they did? Or did you immediately see them as an enemy and assume ulterior motives? Were you willing to change your own position, or were you absolutely certain you were right? If you were offended, did you take it upon yourself to humiliate someone in public, or did you use discernment and address the issue when you were self-regulated? I'm sure you can guess how most people will answer those questions, myself included. Part of the equation is self-management, and we'll talk about that in chapter 4. Be patient with yourself and others as you try on new ideas about conflict and experiment with new methods to manage it.

Remember this: disagreement doesn't ruin relationships; disrespect does. So, we must build conflict capacity so that we learn how to disagree without disrespecting.

Expanding Conflict Capacity

Expanding conflict capacity is about the ability to stay engaged in a difficult conversation, stay present to a high-conflict personality, and build enough self-awareness to create space or set a boundary before getting triggered into old dysfunctional patterns. Just like expanding your physical capabilities such as aerobic capacity, strength, or stamina, building conflict capacity requires conditioning, discipline, and deliberate practice, which enables you to withstand the storms instead of avoiding, appeasing, or aggression.

Building conflict capacity requires you to give up what has made you comfortable up to this point. When it comes to building conflict capacity, comfort is not a requirement. In fact, the biggest barrier to building conflict capacity (outside of cultural influences) is the commitment to comfort. When it comes to building capacity, you must be willing to recognize dysfunctional patterns within yourself. This is extremely uncomfortable. The benefit is once you recognize your own dysfunctional behaviors, you'll be fully equipped to recognize them in the organization.

—————— Recognizing Dysfunctional Patterns ——————

The ability to spot dysfunctional patterns inside your organization can help you pinpoint mismanagement that's leading to the organizational problems. In short, just because you think you understand the problem doesn't mean you understand the cause of the problem.

I sat across from an executive team of a private practice medical clinic at lunch as we talked about all the poor performers who weren't measuring up. When I asked for names, behaviors, and specifics, no one on the executive team could say specifically who, or what was happening. Since the defined problem was "directors who needed to be micromanaged, which resulted in wasted executive time," I suggested we start measuring the amount of time executives spent on managing what their directors should be managing. The CEO didn't like that idea. He said, "We don't want people to think we are nitpicking."

"They won't even know we're measuring it. It's just to get a baseline to see how much time executives are spending doing the directors' jobs," I reassured him. He abruptly changed the subject and summoned the waiter to bring the bill. From my perspective, this is an example of a huge blind spot—avoiding that which is difficult to talk about today without realizing the future consequences. In an organization, the problems you can identify are problems you can fix, and the problems you misidentify equal continued frustration. Mismanagement happens when we don't know how to define the real problem or when we avoid it because we don't want to nitpick, hurt feelings, or seem like a micromanager.

A former client who worked as an HR leader in a large health-care organization wrote to me when she realized the detrimental effects of avoiding conflict.

> I'm just about at the end of a yearlong process of managing a disruptive employee. This situation ended up with lawyers involved and should reach a settlement today. It's been a long and painful process, as this employee had been tolerated for 18 years. This employee was occasionally talked to, but since she was considered a "high performer," she was allowed to carry on, hurting patients, families, and staff along the way, as well as creating chaos in her wake of disruption. The entire process has taken a toll on me, my team, and the employee. I didn't realize how hard emotionally and mentally it would really be.

It's difficult to learn the lessons of avoidance because the pain usually doesn't happen immediately. There's always a lag time between the avoidance, the justification, and the result.

——————— Three Dysfunctional Behaviors ———————

The three dysfunctional behaviors that leaders use to avoid discomfort are avoidance, appeasing, and aggression. Avoiders say "We're all adults" and "I shouldn't have to tell them." Appeasers justify high-conflict behavior because "they are a high performer" or "they have seniority." Aggressors retaliate and say "I didn't ask you to work here. Find another job."

Some leaders put off (avoid) difficult conversations because they're afraid of their own aggression, they don't want to make someone cry, or they view themselves as a "nice leader."

Yelling at an employee (aggression) won't improve their performance or build trust, but some leaders do it anyway. The release of anger feels good in the moment and dissipates some of the discomfort.

We tell a high-driving salesman we'll consider the product *next year* (appeasing) to get him off the phone. We tell people what they want to hear instead of engaging in a tiring conversation where they might pick an argument.

When you think about it, it's all avoidance . . . the avoidance of feelings, the avoidance of furthering the conversation, the avoidance of personal responsibility, and the avoidance of personal growth. The purpose of avoidance is to escape discomfort, or in the case of aggression, it's a way to release the buildup of discomfort. Let's look at avoidance in its purest form, and then I'll address appeasing and aggression.

Avoiding

Some leaders know they avoid and readily admit they hate conflict. The rest of us don't realize how much we chose comfort over accountability. Case in point: Are you eager to step on the scale after a weekend of binge eating? Me neither. But the point is, the facts are what they are, whether you know it or not. If you have a nonperforming salesman who isn't making rain, you can avoid having an accountability conversation. In that case you're choosing comfort before growth for yourself and the nonperformer.

If there's a bully employee in your department, you may deny it, but the bully is still creating toxicity that's about to explode— whether you know it or not. Ask yourself this: Am I walking on eggshells to avoid the bully? Are you avoiding because they are a good performer otherwise? Figuring out why you aren't addressing the issue is half the battle. Looking to the future is a great motivator. What happens if you keep avoiding? Choosing small comforts in this moment often means accepting crisis in the future.

A big excuse managers have for not having a conversation is "I already know what they're going to say." The fact is, they don't know because the conversation hasn't yet been had. What they do know is their past experiences, but when we make these assumptions, we're choosing a *past experience* over a *future possibility*. This habit of "already knowing" is costly to our personal and professional growth. You have to stop focusing on your past and focus forward for your growth. You owe it to yourself, to your employee, and to your organization. Denial and justifications only make things worse in the long run. You're going to have to climb Mud Hill someday, and it might as well be today.

Appeasing

The distinction between avoiding and appeasing is subtle: when you avoid, employees are in the dark. They can't tell if you've forgotten or if you're just afraid to have the conversation. When you appease, employees might think you're nice, or they think you agree when you don't; they think you're interested when you're not. Appeasing is telling someone what they want to hear to get the issue off your plate. If you're a "people person," it feels good to see their eyes sparkle when you tell them something they want to hear. In the end, appeasing erodes trust. How many times has your own boss said something like "Good idea! I'll get back to you" but they never did?

Let's explore appeasing. Suppose you disagree with a colleague, but instead of saying "I disagree" and opening up for dialogue, you say, "You have some excellent points, but I have a meeting. Let's discuss it later." Do you really circle back to discuss later, or is it more convenient to let it slip into the dark?

Most of us use appeasing at least some of the time—for example, when you don't want to let someone down when they ask you to work on a project, be on a board, volunteer for a committee, or do whatever with them. You feel honored, but your insides are screaming "NOOOOO!" But—you want them to like you. You don't have the energy for listening to them try to convince you, so you say yes. Saying yes felt good in the moment, but after the high wears off, you feel resentful and misaligned. You decide to back out later.

You just have to create a little white lie that they'll buy into: Your mother is sick. Your teenager is having a breakdown. Your car is in the shop, and you don't want to hold up the project. "Maybe next time," you say with feigned regret in your voice. All of these behaviors compensate for the discomfort you feel when your decisions are misaligned.

Aggression

Then there's aggression. Aggression ranges from behaviors such as eye-rolling, the silent treatment, dirty looks, innuendos, sarcasm, telling someone off, putting someone in their place in front of others, name-calling, threats, voice-raising, fist-pounding, rage, and violence. I'll be transparent here. I've had to work on eye-rolling and sarcasm, and I've raised my voice plenty of times. I find I'm most aggressive when I've been fretting about something for too long and I've had the conversation in my head and not with the other person. Just ask my husband. He'll confirm.

Remember my boss that I told you about in the previous chapter? He didn't play games, and he didn't undermine, eye-roll, or give dirty looks. No, he was straightforward. He was rude and defensive. He seemed to take any complaint as a personal threat rather than interpreting a complaint as an employee caring about what's going on. He used discounting remarks rather than really listening to complaints.

Aggression can be a sign that the individual has reached their capacity. They've probably been stewing about something for quite a while, and their emotions are boiling over. Or they're holding grudges they haven't resolved, or their physical needs aren't being met and they're exhausted, hungry, or overworked. When we're at capacity, we use the one or two tools in our toolbox to manage conflict: shaming, intimidating, or some other tactic.

What's interesting is that aggressive types often think they're good at addressing conflict, much like the unseasoned managers I spoke about earlier. They say things like "The buck stops here." *What they really mean is that they know how to avoid real conversations without it being called avoidance.* The point is, they're every bit as uncomfortable with conflict as the person who avoids or appeases; they just have a different method of operation.

Once I noticed these patterns, my goal was to understand the root cause of conflict mismanagement. I used to think the pattern was due to lack of skills development. This is when I would go into an organization and provide what was requested: a workshop. The workshop would work for a while, but the patterns would creep back in, or at worst, a manager would try to course correct an employee only to be overridden by their director.

No matter what kind of training is offered, skills development alone won't override a culture where senior leaders override their managers' decision-making. Top leaders sometimes think they need to micromanage because their managers are in the weeds, but there's a reason—the culture. On the flip side, even when the culture supports accountable conversations, the lack of skills development can cause some messy course corrections. If a nice manager in a supportive culture that offers skills development simply doesn't have the inner fortitude and courage, problems naturally seep in. So, what's at the root of avoidance? Lack of experience, skills development, character, or personality? It's the lack of conflict capacity.

———— Building Conflict Capacity ————

Building conflict capacity is more than skills development, temperament, experience, or possessing the right DiSC score on a personality assessment. Building conflict capacity has three distinct but overlapping elements: inner, outer, and culture. If you have only one out of the three, you won't be very effective; two out of three can be beneficial; but when you have all three, you'll excel at dealing with conflict. Think of a Venn diagram with three circles overlapping (see figure 2).

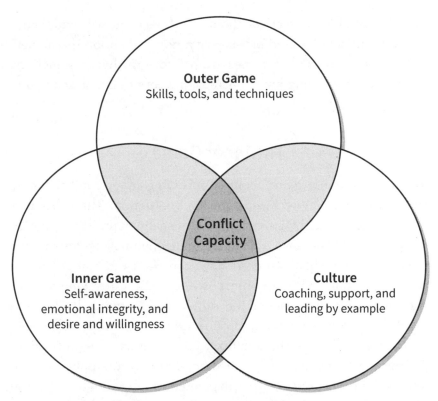

FIGURE 2. Venn diagram of conflict capacity

The inner game is about clarity, alignment, and decision-making, the foundation of which includes self-awareness, self-regulation, emotional integrity, desire, intention, and willingness.

The outer game is about skills development and results made manifest through tools, techniques, and deliberate practice.

The culture is about senior leaders leading by example, policies that reinforce desired behaviors, alignment to a stated set of values. This is followed by a commitment to leadership development with coaching and support to make the behaviors stick, followed by accountable conversations when they don't.

The sweet spot of conflict capacity is when all three circles overlap and where you are building an expansive capacity for managing and overcoming conflict. Without all three, you will experience wasted time and lowered productivity, not to mention the anxiety and mental drama that comes from knowing there's something more but not knowing how to achieve it. Let's talk first about winning the inner game.

The Inner Game

Winning the inner game requires resolving inner conflict before trying to course correct a person or a situation. That's because the first conflict is the inner conflict—misalignment. Misalignment happens when you have a divided mind, when beliefs don't match behaviors, and when you don't have the clarity to make the best decisions. You think the conflict is about the tardy employee or the aggressive coworker or the unreasonable senior leader. You want them to change, but you don't want to risk the relationship by having what might be a difficult conversation. You can't afford to lose them even if they are mediocre. They're the only one who knows this part of the job. They're going through a rough patch. You have valid reasons for avoiding the conversation. In addition, you're a leader who cares. If you didn't care, there wouldn't even be a conflict at all. You'd have the conversation. You'd move on. You'd ignore it. You'd compensate. You'd fire someone. You'd leave. You'd speak up. And you wouldn't be all that concerned about what happened, but good leaders care on many levels. We care about our career, and we're afraid to say something to jeopardize it. We care about how we come off to the employee when we have to have a difficult conversation. We care about what people think. We care about the consequences of speaking up, and we care about the consequences of not speaking up. We care about our sense of security. We care about our self-esteem and self-image. We care about being understood, and we worry about being misunderstood.

The first conflict is that you want two things at the same time that are in opposition—you're in a state of misalignment internally.

You want to have a conversation, but you don't want to upset the employee. You want to promote the key player, but the company honors seniority first. You want to be available, but you need to close the open door before it becomes a revolving door. Wanting two things at the same time is exhausting and takes up a lot of mental energy. You feel indecisive, confused, all over the place. Here's why: you're indecisive because you're misaligned, and you're misaligned because you aren't clear on your values, or if you are clear, you don't know how to make distinctions that guide your decision-making. Your desires, drives, and demands are in opposition, which at the core is an internal conflict. To win the inner game, you must resolve your inner conflicts first.

Resolving Inner Conflict

Resolving inner conflict requires three things: self-awareness, a strong values system, and discernment. Let me give you an example of how these three qualities work together; then we'll break it down.

I'm self-aware enough to know when I'm about to reach my capacity. I've become aware of how my physical body feels when I'm getting impatient. When I'm tired and haven't given myself a break, I become impatient, and my behaviors are not something I like about myself. I get a little short with others, or I interrupt, or I might let out a sigh, just a little hint to hurry the other person who has become an obstacle in my mind. It's as if I lose my capacity to care. I want what I want. But these behaviors, while they feel good in the moment, are in opposition to something I *value* deeply—something that makes me a good coach and a critical thinker—a skill I call "radical listening," the ability to be present when it's difficult. We'll explore more about radical listening in chapters 6 and 7.

Now that we have talked about the opposing drives, desires, and demands that create inner conflict, let's look at *discernment*. I'm discerning enough to tell you that my impatience has also served me many times. My sense of urgency helps me to get things done and strive for more efficiency. So then is impatience good or bad? It all depends.

The discernment comes when you ask the question: *Does this serve me now?* This is how you use self-awareness, values, and discernment to resolve the inner conflict and make better decisions about who you want to be in the world.

I've had to create several habits to manage my own sense of urgency and make distinctions about when it serves me and when it doesn't. The icing on the cake for me is when someone thanks me for being patient. That's when I started noticing that I had become a creative force in my own life to change from the inside out.

The inner game requires you to be in integrity with yourself. You have to admit when you're in over your head. You need to know when you're not capable in the moment so that you can set a boundary or an appropriate time to become fully present. Once you tell yourself the truth, you can be in integrity with others.

—————— How to Improve Your Inner Game ——————

Notice how energy processes through your body. For example, when you get angry, what happens? Does your neck get hot, or does your heart rate increase? Next, notice your thoughts. What are you telling yourself about your anger? Are you blaming the other person? Are you ashamed of yourself because you think anger is wrong? Awareness of your body is one of the first steps to getting honest about what you're experiencing, but you have to be discerning. What's causing your reactions? Could it be something else you're unaware of?

I would be remiss if I didn't mention a pattern I've seen: a belief that their anger, impatience, and negativity is a character defect that can be overcome by trying to become a "better person." Believe me, I have taken that journey and it's a long and winding dark road. What works is to increase awareness of your physiological needs.

For example, it's a lot easier to be a "better person" if your needs are met and you're well fed and well rested. Recently, I purchased an Oura ring, which gives me information about my sleep patterns and any problems of getting enough deep sleep and rapid eye movement to clean out the brain and make me more effective. I can tell you how much of a "better person" I am when I don't eat too late, when I go to bed at the same time and have excellent recovery. As leaders we're also responsible for our energy systems and our health because being healthy in mind, body, and spirit makes us better decision-makers, more-critical thinkers, and ultimately better leaders. Get whatever technology, tools, and other support you need to become the best version of yourself. Knowledge used is power. Here are three steps to increase your emotional integrity:

Step 1: For one day, set a timer to go off every hour for the entire day. Stop and take a breath, and then be still and mentally scan your body. No multitasking, no talking on the phone, and no reading emails. Take two minutes for yourself. Notice your heart rate, your shoulders, your neck, and your stomach. Notice your breathing. Is it fast, slow, shallow, or deep? Are you thirsty or hungry? Are you holding tension? Shift your posture, and reset your clock. Keep doing this for the rest of the day. Then, repeat again tomorrow. Get good at knowing your physical self.

Step 2: Name one pattern you have that you'd like to change— for example, impatience, appeasing, or sarcasm. What happens that triggers you into a defensive or avoidant stance? If you can name it, you can change it. Make a commitment to stop blaming the other person, and instead just notice what trips your trigger. Awareness is always the first step. You aren't trying to change yourself or change them. You aren't judging yourself. You are just observing. Your goal is just to notice what rubs you wrong. It might be when someone interrupts. It might be tardiness. It might be when someone is condescending.

Now, name that pattern you have and what triggers your behavior.

Step 3: Ask yourself, *Is this serving me now?* This exercise is likely to make you uncomfortable. It won't feel like you are doing enough to matter. It will feel more like personal development than real leadership development. Your brain will tell you all kinds of things like "I don't have time for this" or "This is just silly." That's just a sign that you have work to do. Self-awareness work is hard work. Winning the inner game requires a desire to learn, more than a desire to be comfortable. You have to show up for yourself first before you show up for others. You desire to learn so much that you're willing to look in the mirror and know your strengths and weaknesses.

Evidence You're Improving

Here's the evidence of improvement: First, you'll notice your feelings and behaviors *after* the fact. Next, you'll catch yourself *during* the act, even though you can't control it. Finally, you see the trigger *before* it happens, and it's like slow motion. There's enough space to make a change.

The tendency for most of us is to judge ourselves for not being enough. I certainly have had enough self-judgment to last a lifetime, but I find it more helpful just to admit when I'm hungry, tired, or simply needing a break. I'm prouder of myself when I tell myself the truth about my capabilities instead of trying to push past when there's no more gas left in the tank. Telling yourself the truth is required. You can only be as honest as your level of self-awareness, and I guarantee if you deceive yourself on a regular basis, you deceive others even if it's unintentional. Winning the inner game is about cleaning up the inside first before helping or controlling other people. Most of what we do to avoid conflict is simply a means to stay comfortable, and when it comes to building conflict capacity, comfort is not a requirement.

———————————— The Outer Game ————————————

The second part of building conflict capacity is what I call the outer game. As I said, the outer game is about skills development and results you get due to techniques and tools that you deliberately practice. You can take a skills development course in listening and you'll learn intellectually some methods to become a better listener; however, if you don't have enough emotional integrity, stamina, and self-awareness to actually practice and embody the new skill, you'll have knowledge but not the behavior. That's where coaching comes in to create accountability for practicing the new skills, but this is the exception rather than the rule.

Most people start with the outer game. They take a communication skills course and call it a day. Those who really make the most of their self-directed learning continue to practice until they notice a shift in their own behaviors and thinking. The most useful practice is to work on these skills with a group of like-minded, growth-oriented peers where you can get support and mentor each other. The reason I started by describing the inner game is because skills development without self-awareness, discernment, and practice will go only so far. You'll get book knowledge but not the behavior. Behaviors come from the *grind* of deliberate practice to change the old, ingrained patterns that connected in your brain a long time ago and worked for you until now.

Some of the skills leaders need to learn include listening, redirecting nonproductive conversations, overcoming resistance, uncovering objections, coaching to empowerment, setting boundaries, and having accountability conversations, to name a few. Most of these skills are offered in this book. In the end, it's not about the *skills*, it's about the *results* the skills give you, so let's talk about results here and skills later in chapter 7. Every leader needs to know how to get these results:

➡ Focus everyone in the same direction.

➡ Clarify objectives and outcomes.

→ Course correct inappropriate behavior.

→ Coach employees to improved performance.

→ Navigate change and uncertainty.

→ De-escalate arguments and petty grievances.

The bottom line is that skills serve the purpose of improving the organizational outcomes, whether it's increasing sales, improving productivity, reducing costs, improving collaboration, elevating morale, or simply making the workplace a better place to work, thus retaining employees and growing the business. Skills development that doesn't lead to *embodiment* is just a notch above entertainment. I'm often quoted for saying "Get a clown and a pizza and it will save you more money." Real skill development needs to be an investment in people and in outcomes. Unless someone is ultra-self-directed, real skill development usually requires more than a virtual training or a live workshop; it requires coaching groups, mentoring, measurable behavior change, and accountability.

The Culture

"Culture" is a buzz word overly used in leadership conversations, the definition of which is rarely agreed upon or understood. Some say culture is a set of beliefs that govern behavior. Others see culture as "the way we do things around here." To introduce a greater understanding about culture, I'll share this definition given to me (during a phone call) with the top thought leader on culture, Dr. Edgar Schein, who said, "Culture is what a group learns as its way of surviving and both getting along internally and solving its problems externally. Culture is formed by external and internal forces. What's often missing from discussions about culture is the understanding of how the external environment influences culture." We will talk more about the environment in chapter 5, but let's take a peek at the external and internal forces within each culture.

─────────── External and Internal Forces ───────────

Think about what happened around the world when an *external and invisible force* known as the COVID-19 pandemic changed the ways we thought about work and eventually the way in which we work across the entire globe. Businesses that viewed themselves as brick and mortar allowed their employees to work from home, when it would have been unimaginable before this outside environmental influence. An invisible virus became the outside force that changed the culture of work. To survive, businesses had to innovate. Restaurants had to figure out how to turn parking lots into outdoor seating.

From a global perspective, the pandemic influenced values and behaviors. To survive, people started wearing masks, social distancing, and practicing extreme hygiene. Grocery stores ran out of toilet paper and hand sanitizers as people placed high value on what was in the past viewed as a mundane necessity. The increased demand for toilet paper, masks, and sanitizers gave some businesses more opportunity due entirely to outside influences, not because of their own marketing, their own collaboration, or their own teamwork. Other high-touch businesses like hotels, dance studios, concerts, and massage therapists shut down, not because of the lack of teamwork, poor marketing strategies, or inexperience, but because of outside influences that were outside of their control. And because of the uncertainty about when things would finally get back to normal, combined with lack of trust in experts and the media, major conflicts erupted between friends of opposing political and social orientations.

Fear and uncertainty always affect the culture, whether it's the culture of a small business, an enterprise, a community, a nation, or the entire globe. So, what does this have to do with conflict capacity and leadership? There will always be unforeseen forces that affect culture, but leaders have a measure of control over the inner environment, and they can develop skills to ensure the organization survives.

The culture (what we do to get along and survive on the inside) must be a fit for a new leader, no matter what their title or role. The culture as well as the environmental influences of a particular organization and industry at large are about how leaders at the top view and respond to conflict. For example, if executives avoid bad news and difficult conversations, don't expect the newly promoted director to right the ship. They won't be supported, and as a result, the new leader learns quickly to align with the example in front of them. If managers aren't making decisions, it could be cultural: they're following examples at the top, or their past decisions have been overridden to keep peace. Some cultures can be very dysfunctional, yet during low-stress times, everything works well. They get along because they avoid looking at any bad news, or they promote only family members to leadership positions, whether they have the skills or not, but change, as an outside force, shifts the culture from one that worked to one that is teetering on chaos.

I've seen family-owned businesses that had been operating for over thirty years and the owners didn't have a good understanding of the financials, weren't up to date technologically, and had never gotten around to creating a policy manual or creating standard operating procedures. They relied on the good nature and loyalty of their workers, never giving them a raise and getting them to work overtime because of the "friendly culture." Eventually, when owners desire to leave the business, they hire an outsider to right the ship and get the business ready to sell. There's a lot less getting along and a lot more conflict between the employees, who feel betrayed. In these instances, the owners don't really understand their own culture, the external environment, or change management.

What You Can Do Now

Look at both the internal and external factors that shape your culture. What do you have control over, and where must you adapt? Being able to explain this to your employees can help you to create better collaboration, rather than feeling like it's all up to you or that your powers are unlimited. Next, do an inventory on your inner game. Where do you have work to do? For most of us, it's about learning how to build space between stimulus and response and to get out of avoiding, appeasing, or aggression. The outer game is about practice until you get perfect. The next time you get caught off guard, don't appease and don't get aggressive. Instead, say something like, "You've caught me off guard and at a bad time. I'm interested to hear more, but I need to set a date for Thursday at two." Then get the conversation on the calendar, and prepare yourself so that you have the capacity to handle the emotions. Always set boundaries when the conversation escalates. You can always start over when you've had rest and time to think. It gets easier with time, but when you're learning, don't allow yourself to be caught off guard. Take charge of your time and mental energy.

Conflict capacity includes the awareness to know you've hit your limit mentally and emotionally. To build conflict capacity, practice expanding your tolerance for uncertainty or discomfort while skillfully navigating the complexities of conflict. In summary, the inner game is the self-awareness, values, and discernment that enable you to withstand the storm. The outer game is skill sets, deliberate practice, and accountability. *The culture includes the internal and external influences that inform how people work together.* Leaders get the best results when the culture intersects with their inner game and outer game.

———————————— **Reflection** ————————————

1. What is your default pattern when faced with conflict?

2. What triggers conflict in you?

3. How does your organization's culture support you as a leader?

4. What skill do you need to become more conflict capable?

2

Identity:
The Price of Being Too Nice

*The story that's been resolved
no longer needs to be told.*

Alisha struggled in her new executive director role. She found it difficult to think of herself as a boss when just a few short weeks before she was working alongside the coworkers who now reported to her. Alisha wasn't prepared for dealing with conflict, making tough calls, and initiating difficult conversations around performance or behavior. When Alisha called me, I could hear the uncertainty and stress in her voice.

There's a certain death that comes with a new identity. You have to leave the idea of who you were to become who you need to be. Alisha said, "Without an orientation, this transition has been like having a file cabinet full of folders dumped on the floor to see what still belongs, what needs to be thrown out, and what needs to be added." Alisha had to make the mental shift of going from "one of us" to "one of them." The first conflict for Alisha was an internal conflict: seeing herself differently.

The identity shift from peer to leader is difficult. Identity is one of the invisible elements of the inner game: who you think you are and how you see yourself. Alisha didn't have much time to prepare for leadership. She didn't attend any classes and had no formal mentoring and no certifications that had to be completed before being crowned a leader. She simply applied for the opening and got it. One day she's a colleague, and the next day she's a boss. Alisha was experiencing an identity crisis.

But Alisha had a more pressing problem than just her identity. That problem was Tony, a seasoned veteran who Alisha viewed as unmanageable and uncooperative. Tony had influence over the other employees. From Alisha's perspective, Tony was the ringleader, a bully who influenced others, and she didn't know what to do. "I've talked to Tony a thousand times, and nothing changes," Alisha said. When Alisha first called me to inquire about my services, I thought maybe the difficulty between her and Tony had to do with seniority, jealousy, or some sort of turf war based on promotion. So, I tested my initial assumption. "Do you think Tony is jealous of your position?" I asked. After a thoughtful pause, Alisha responded. "No, I was the only one who applied, so it isn't jealousy. No one else wanted this job," she answered. Alisha didn't know leadership would be so difficult. She wasn't prepared for dealing with conflict, making tough calls, and initiating difficult conversations around performance or behavior. She certainly didn't know how to hold employees accountable, and she didn't know how to deal with a pot stirrer like Tony. Alisha assumed that having authority would make Tony easier to manage, but Alisha was just too nice. She allowed excuses. She covered for employees' mistakes. She made exceptions, and being nice was costing her. Let's look at how leaders fall into dysfunctional behaviors due to the influence of identity, personal narrative, and culture. Then we'll look at how to create a new leadership identity as a leader who has the capacity to handle difficult situations and even difficult personalities.

—— Three Dysfunctional Leadership Identities ——

Overly nice leaders often create unintended and unnecessary team drama because their overriding priority is to be liked and to avoid conflict. They try to become best friends, a hero, or a hands-off leader. For an easy snapshot, I've outlined the behaviors of a leader that can cause dysfunction. Most of us can spot our own tendencies in these three archetypes.

Best-Friend Leaders

The honeymoon period works well in the beginning, but reality hits when internal conflict between employees requires the best friend to choose sides. The best-friend leader cares more about being liked and making employees feel good than they do about aligning with the mission of the organization; therefore, they forget their leadership role and behave in ways that are misaligned with being a leader.

→ Getting distracted by listening to hearsay

→ Avoiding direct conversations

→ Being unable to identify the root problems

→ Blaming upper management for decisions

→ Having global conversations about individual problems

Hero Leaders

Leaders who love to *help* can easily cross the line from helping to heroism. They create dependency by always having the answer. Overhelping can be interpreted as micromanagement by employees seeking autonomy.

→ Being unable or unwilling to delegate

→ Taking credit instead of giving credit

→ Fixing everyone else's problems

➡ Allowing the open door to become a revolving door

➡ Having overly dependent employees

Hands-Off Leaders

The hands-off leader is not a micromanager—just the opposite. The pendulum has swung too far in the other direction, and the hands-off leader is unaware of looming problems. There's plenty of trust and support, just no accountability.

➡ Brushing complaints under the carpet

➡ Changing the structure before talking to the individuals

➡ Failing to assist lower-level leaders when problems occur

➡ Not seeing the drama until it has gotten out of control

➡ Being unable to see the role leaders play in the team's drama

New leaders often get in over their heads, and when they do, they hide their problems from upper management because they don't want to appear incompetent. These new leaders need support, but there's fear about disrupting the status quo. *Here is some north star advice for all leaders:* Let your boss know when you're in over your head. Never blindside upper-level leaders by problems that get out of hand. If you don't know how to make a strategic decision, your first step is to document your situation and what you've tried. Then go to your senior-level leader to get some advice and mentoring. You're still going to be responsible for fixing the problem. You aren't asking to be bailed out. You're simply reporting what's happening and seeking wisdom. Your boss will be thankful.

I asked Alisha if her senior executives would respect her decision-making should she decide to let them know what she was up against and if she were able to set some standards and hold Tony accountable. To my surprise, Alisha said they would. So now that I knew the culture was intact, I knew it was likely that Alisha's obstacle was her inner game—her leadership identity.

Alisha's focus on bad employee behavior kept her from looking at her own dysfunctional patterns of behavior. Alisha was divided internally. Remember my definition of conflict: opposing drives, desires, and demands. Alisha had two arrows going in opposite directions.

Alisha wanted Tony to change, but she also wanted to be perceived as nice. She was trying to win Tony over by appeasing and avoiding, but it wasn't working. She knew she needed to hold Tony accountable, but she was afraid Tony would cause even more trouble. Alisha also believed the problem was outside of herself.

—————— Why People Do What They Do ——————

Almost every leader thinks the root problem is the employee. That's because there is *visible evidence to see*. The employee keeps coming in late. The employee is a bully. The employee is insubordinate. The employee stirs up other employees. The employee isn't performing. The employee isn't documenting correctly. The employee isn't making sales quota. The employee, the employee, the employee.

Why do people do what they do? Because it works. The employee is doing what works for them. To be clear, employees aren't necessarily looking for ways to disrupt their managers; it's just that as human beings we all behave in ways that work for us, and we continue to do what we do until there's some reason to change.

The one with clarity navigates the ship. But I'm ahead of myself. We'll talk more about leadership clarity in the next chapter. The point is, people do what works for them, and if you have avoided addressing the issue, they will continue to do what they want.

To quote my friend and former client Heather Joyner, a director in a 911 emergency call center and the founder of The PSAP Consulting Group, "The behavior allowed becomes the standard." If Tony instigates drama, Sheena will also do it, then later even your best employee, Raju, will follow suit. In your role as a leader, part of your job is to initiate difficult conversations about behavior and performance. Remember, all employees are watching you.

"But I've told them a thousand times!" Alisha said. Maybe you've said that too. That only means you have allowed the behavior 999 times. I'm joking just a little here. Oh, I know it feels like you've said it a thousand times, but you've probably *only thought* about it a thousand times. Every time you thought about it, you got angry, and you visualized what you'd like to say if you had the courage. But did you say it? Probably not. You're too nice for that. Maybe you had a team meeting—a *global conversation*—when you really needed to talk to just one person.

Have you ever noticed that when you have global team meetings, the one person who needs to get the message doesn't think it applies to them? If you say, "We all need to come in on time and not be tardy," Late Lydia will nod in agreement, totally oblivious that the only reason you brought it up is because of her tardiness. If you tell the entire team to make sure to use good hygiene, that you've had some complaints of foul odor, Stinky Stan won't realize it's he who needs a bath.

A good sign that you've been holding back, avoiding, or appeasing is resentment. If you feel resentment, it's because you let something go on way too long. And if you've let things go on too long, it's probably because you don't really see the power you hold as a leader. When you feel resentment for too long, anger erupts, and when anger erupts, you'll be accused of being aggressive. The very behaviors you have been using to try to keep the peace only increase conflict as time goes by.

Let me check in for a moment. Did anything in this chapter make you angry? I hope not. I've made every single mistake I'm pointing out. As the saying goes, you teach what you need to learn.

Heather learned years ago as the director of a 911 emergency call center that the leader sets the standard. The buck has to stop with you. But there's good news: you can still be polite, respectful, and encouraging while stopping the buck and creating accountability.

In Alisha's case, she called me to ask for a workshop, which told me she thought the problem was outside of herself. She was hoping

I could influence the employees to stop going along with Tony. This happens almost weekly in my world. There's some major problem that's been brewing over several months, or there's a big blow up or team conflict, and a leader calls me . . . hoping I can fix the problem.

It's as if there's some sort of magical wish that if I can come in for about four hours and change all the employees' minds about their drama, they will suddenly be enlightened, and then they will get along. Translated, this means the leader can avoid being uncomfortable by not having to do the dirty work of having difficult conversations that make employees uncomfortable or defensive. Or in the case of cultural misalignment, the less-senior leader hopes that my work will help get the attention and support of the senior executives before she becomes the scapegoat. Unfortunately, it doesn't really work that way unless the senior-level leaders are the ones actually seeking the solution. In that case, they are willing participants and eagerly looking at all levels of leadership in order to make the cultural shifts.

Alisha didn't yet realize that a workshop wouldn't help her employees to suddenly become accountable. Alisha was the only one who could hold employees accountable, but she had to identify with being a leader first.

A person who fully identifies with being a leader would at least try to address performance and behavioral issues. Don't get me wrong, with or without good skills training, there will be mismanagement and mistakes, but the point is, it's leadership identity that drives behavior to initiate performance conversations, whether they actually achieve success.

Identity, Behavior, and Narrative

I said this in my book *Stop Workplace Drama*, and I'll say it again here: the way you see yourself has everything to do with your workplace relationships and how you lead others. Your leadership is grounded in your identity. Identity is your behavior acted out, based on what you tell yourself. If you tell yourself that you're too sensitive to give feedback, then you'll behave in a consistent way with your narrative. Your brain, through a structure called reticular activating system, or RAS for short, will actually look for evidence to support your narrative.

What is a narrative, and where do our narratives originate? you might ask. A narrative is the story that's always going on inside your head. It's what you tell yourself about who you are and why you do certain things. In simplified and practical terms, we human beings seek to make meaning of experiences, past situations, and our relationship to others and to the world. It's the silent voice always communicating with you to become the story by which you live life.

As an exercise, listen to how people describe themselves using "I am," and you will witness part of their narrative. "I am very particular" or "I am organized" or "I'm conflict adverse" or "I'm the type of person who would . . ." and even "That's just the way I am" are all examples of a narrative being spoken. Your narrative is the story you tell yourself and others about yourself to justify your behaviors.

Your narrative forms over time starting with your history and what your authority figures told you about yourself, and your story evolves over time as you grow and experience life. We've all been told things like we are gifted, clumsy, inconsiderate, brilliant, or incompetent. You hear these things when you're too young to think critically. When you are a very young age, your brain is in theta and highly suggestible, so you believe whatever your authority figures tell you about who you are, and then you build upon these stories with your experiences over time.

We rarely question these stories until we have some sort of awakening and are ready to challenge outdated beliefs and make intentional changes. Until then, the stories we believe become the behaviors we act out, whether it's avoiding conversations, being aggressive, manipulating, or being nice at the cost of respect.

In your role as a leader, it's important to understand the power of narrative as it relates to your leadership journey, to managing conflict and influencing others in our divisive world. Here's why: the story you tell is the life you live. The story that has been resolved no longer needs to be told. What we haven't resolved in our lives we continue to talk about, and what we talk about takes up energy, and where we put our energy is where we put our attention, and where we put our attention is what we create. We keep situations alive and create more of what we don't want when our narrative is about unresolved past issues. Greatness is not achieved by rehashing past grievances. As a leader, you can revise your own story and then help others shift their narrative so they can reach their potential. If something is unresolved, there are three pathways: acceptance, forgiveness, and empowerment. Empowerment is recognizing the choices you have today. Anything else is a prison of our own making. Perhaps the reason it's so difficult to dissect our narratives is because our narratives are shaped by culture.

Culture Influences Identity

We are all products of our culture. Here, I'm talking about the broader context of culture, including your personal history; your country of origin; the industries you've worked in; your gender, race, family of origin; and literally every experience you've ever had. These elements shape our narrative of who we are in the world, how we perceive things to work, and what we perceive to be "the truth" of reality. Each individual enters a workplace culture with their own deeply personal experience of culture.

As I said before, workplace culture is not just a set of beliefs that govern behavior. In the workplace, culture is what we do on the inside to get along and survive on the outside. When the senior leaders avoid and cover issues, it's not likely you'll have the confidence to lead from a bold stance. You just wouldn't fit in. And if you get hired as an interim to "right the ship," be warned that you may not be able to override the status quo. You won't be supported if you make it too uncomfortable. You'll be common enemy number one.

When the senior-level leaders aren't clear about the vision, neither will the middle managers be.

No matter who you are, your (personal) culture affects your narrative and thus your behaviors, even when logically your behaviors don't make sense. Do you ever see women walking around in stiletto heels even though it's hard to balance and the shoes hurt? Sure you do. That's because it's part of the cultural conditioning for Western women. It makes no sense. The shoes hurt, and as any orthopedic surgeon will tell you, stiletto heels aren't good for your bones, yet we women want to "look good," and this look is part of business attire for many industries. Watch a presidential inauguration in the US, and you'll see the First Lady walking for miles on concrete in stilettos. Then the following days, watch all the commentary about her attire. Does it really matter? No, but that's culture at work. Let's stay tuned to see how culture evolves when we get a First Gentleman. What will he wear? Will we care enough to talk about it?

What you do depends on how you see yourself. We spend money on tattoos, get our bodies pierced, wear uncomfortable clothes with labels on them, buy cars we can't afford, because we are influenced by marketing and we want to fit into certain cultures. Most of the time we don't realize it's programming. As a human being, you can't escape the fact that culture has shaped your identity regarding gender, race, occupation, interests, politics, and geographics. Your identity, what you hold to be true about yourself, drives your behaviors.

Everyone Has Bias

We are all shaped by culture. What that means is that every single person is biased in some way; it's just a matter of context and quantity. When it comes to cultural bias, unconscious bias, and every other kind of bias, it's best to stop trying to tell others how biased they are and instead come to an agreement that we all have biases.

This puts everyone on equal footing so that we are free to work on ourselves, to explore our own biases first, without carrying the burden of changing everyone else before we've done our inner work.

What a paradox we live in when we see things in others (biases, behaviors, identities) without seeing them in ourselves. Behaviors also influence identity, and behaviors affect culture, but people don't change unless there's a reason to do so. When I've tried to teach behaviors only without helping leaders understand leadership identity, I often see a lot of resistance. It's common to hear "That's just the way I am" and "I want to be authentic to who I am." What this means is there's a story I'm telling myself about what it means to be me; therefore, if you ask me to change a behavior and it "feels inauthentic," then I can't do it; I have no choice and my behaviors are fixed.

The Power of Your Narrative

The only reason behaviors are fixed is because the narrative is about the past and the present instead of a vision of who you want to be in the future. Now if that doesn't excite you, I don't know what will! You can become the leader you want to be by changing your narrative, and that's a lot easier than trying to force behaviors that right now don't align with who you think you are. Even better, whatever biases you have, you can change those too when you create a different narrative! No matter how self-aware you strive to be, in the end the endless quest for higher levels of awareness is a bottomless pit; however, when you intentionally put your awareness on creating a new narrative, you get the structure you need to change your identity, and when you change your identity, you change your life.

When it comes to who you think you are, your identity *always drives* behavior, and culture influences your identity. I have offered training, skills development, and even a blueprint on how to have conversations, yet some leaders still struggle. It isn't that they don't know the skills. In fact, some of them could make an A on a written exam. We all know the answer in a workshop. What motivates new leaders to actually use and embody these skills is *how they think about themselves*. We get very attached to our identities. We need to believe that what we think about ourselves is the final truth. We resist trying on behaviors that don't feel authentic to the narrative we've created. In fact, we even judge other people's intentions and motives based on our own rules, instead of getting curious about them.

Aligned Leadership Identity

When it comes to leadership, it's not only how you see yourself but how others see you as well. For example, you can see yourself as a leader and you can live in a fantasy world of seeing yourself a certain way, but if no one else buys into it, you're going to struggle. It reminds me of a saying in a quirky little book called *The Lazy Man's Guide to Enlightenment*, where the author, Thaddeus Golas, says, "Whatever you say is true, but only for you and those who agree with you." The point here is that leadership is not just a title, it's a state of being that observably is agreed upon by others—that is, they follow you, they report to you, they are influenced by you, or they get your guidance in some way. In order for you to be a leader, others have to see you that way too, including your boss, the one who crowned you leader, and the ones who agree to be influenced and guided by you. Let's look at three different realities when it comes to leadership.

> **Reality 1: You see yourself as a leader, and others agree.**
> There's no problem with this reality. You identify with being a leader, and others agree that you are a leader. What you say goes. You are the final decision maker. You offer guidance and advice. You take responsibility for the final results. You influence others. You were selected by others who said, "You

have leadership qualities." Your qualities, skills, and attributes align with what is needed to be a leader in your particular organization.

Reality 2: You see yourself as a leader, but others don't. You have the title of leader, and you have some authority, but if your employees see you as too bossy, they don't see you as a leader. They see you as a tyrant. You're too aggressive, unapproachable, and unreasonable. Your employees see boss but not leader. This may be a conflict of definition. There's some sort of misalignment regarding your reality and other people's reality. You have some work to do to build trust and create collaboration. Or suppose you don't have the title but think you should. Your boss doesn't see the qualities you know you have. You haven't been recognized; therefore, even though you are well liked, you haven't proven that you are leadership material. You also have some work to do. You have to find out how your own boss views leadership and what's required to be a leader in your organization so that you can align to that definition.

Reality 3: You do not see yourself as a leader, but others do. You just got promoted, you have a new title and new responsibilities, and you want to be a leader, but you don't feel like one. Someone else saw something within you that illustrated leadership qualities, but your narrative hasn't yet caught up. I'll never forget my transformation from blue-collar worker to professional. My self-image had not elevated with my accomplishments and skills. I had a friend who used to say, "If you could just see yourself through my eyes." I was stuck in an old identity based on the past and had not taken ownership that I had created a whole new life experience.

Maybe you just got the promotion because, like Alisha, you applied for it, you had the seniority, and no one else wanted it. If you want to succeed as a leader, you need to start owning the identity of leader and working on the skills; otherwise, you will have the title only but not the respect.

—— Building Your Personal Leadership Identity ——

Even if your organization doesn't offer leadership development, you can still work on your own identity for the purpose of increasing your capabilities. Here's a step-by-step process for building your leadership identity: commit to awareness, create a personal definition of leadership, claim your values, envision your future self, and build self-trust.

Step 1: Know Your Story

Become aware of your narrative identity, the story you tell yourself about who you are. Who do you say you are? Which of the three leadership realities are you living in? Do others see you as a leader but you haven't caught up to that identity? Do you see yourself as a leader but others don't take you seriously? Take a look at your leadership behaviors. Make a list of behaviors that you aren't proud of—for example, using sarcasm, avoiding, procrastinating. Now look at how your identity shapes those behaviors. What were you thinking that led to the action you took or didn't take? I'm not asking you to beat yourself up but to embrace the facts as they are now so you can change them. You can't change what you don't acknowledge, but clarity can change any situation. This awareness may not feel good initially, but it will help you speed up the process of creating a new leadership identity. How do you describe yourself? Here are some prompts you can use for reflection or for discussion in a book club:

1. When it comes to managing conflict, as a leader, I am . . .

2. As a leader I describe myself as . . .

3. A quality I'm proud of as a leader is . . .

4. An area where I need to improve is . . .

5. The attributes I have that help me be a good leader are . . .

6. Where I lack courage is when . . .

7. What I tell myself when I'm struggling is . . .

To increase self-awareness, consider writing in a leadership-identity journal. Observe your behaviors over the course of a month. Jot down what you see. Does what you see align with the highest version of who you want to be, or do you have work to do?

Step 2: Create a Personal Definition for Leadership

Many who take on the role of leader don't have a good working definition of leadership. Managers who have been in leadership positions for decades often tell me, "I haven't thought much about leadership." The more you think about leadership, the easier it will be to identify with being a leader. That's because with an elevated awareness of what leadership means to you, you can design your own leadership identity instead of relying on fate or guessing or what you've always done. You set yourself up for success not only in the organization you work for now but for future opportunities.

If the organization has a definition for leadership, start there. If the definition is on the walls but not in the halls, observe where the definition is misaligned with the behaviors you notice. This is a first indication that the culture may prevent you from leading the way you want to lead. Think about this question for a moment: What do leaders do? They guide, mentor, influence, support, inspire, and offer feedback and course correction. They also direct resources, create reports, and handle other managerial responsibilities.

Compare your organization's definition with the definition you create for yourself and see where they align and where they clash. My definition for leadership is this: if leadership is about anything, it's about alignment, and alignment is about focusing energy.

Alignment to what? you ask. Alignment to your desired outcomes and stated values. You can't achieve alignment if you don't know what you're aligning to. Clarity comes first. Once you have clarity about your desired result, your actions, thoughts, and initiatives "align" to that end result, not to any means possible, but in harmony with established values. That's what alignment means in the context of my work.

How this definition has helped me is to realize that in conversations, it's up to the leader to guide the direction of the conversation. If (according to my definition) leadership is about alignment, the conversation has to be aligned with higher values of integrity, personal responsibility, and compassion, with the end result being, for example, a 15 percent increase in sales. If the conversation gets off course and becomes irresponsible, abusive, or full of blame, then as a leader, I know I have allowed the misdirection. My focus in anything I lead is about clarity and alignment, and this has been the cornerstone of my work. Because of this definition that I operate from, I can tell when there's a lack of clarity and alignment.

Step 3: Claim Your Values

When I'm listening to others, it doesn't take long for me to know what their top three or four core values are because they will say things like, "I want to be fair" and "It's my goal to create autonomy on my team." Very often, though, it's difficult for the leader to state immediately their top three to five values. Saying your values out loud gives you a very clear picture of how to shape your own behavior and leadership identity. It goes without saying that every value has a price to pay—there are requirements to align with the value. One of my top values is personal responsibility. How this has shaped my behavior is when I find myself complaining, I realize I'm probably seeing myself as a victim or blaming someone or something. It gives me a compass to course correct my behavior of complaining and blaming. Another value for me is empowerment. We all have choices, and until we recognize our choices, we unwillingly become a victim to the cultural influences, the flavor of the day as given to us by the media, or the influence of our friends and families. Personal values serve as a compass to keep you heading in the right direction or to identify when you're off course.

For example, let's say you really hate conflict, but you need to initiate a performance conversation that you think won't be received well. You don't want to hurt feelings or see the other person become defensive. Your top two values are kindness and personal responsibility. You are in an inner conflict, which at first glance seems like a conflict of values. Can you be kind and still require personal responsibility? It doesn't feel kind to deliver the kind of message you're about to deliver. But you know that it's kind to tell someone the truth so they can course correct and not be caught off guard. Because you believe in personal responsibility, you give your employee the chance to step up, instead of rescuing them. This is how you embody your own values, shape your leadership identity, and do what is required to align with your values.

We humans have a deep need to be congruent. Naming your values helps you commit to being congruent. Personal values tell you if you're working for the right organization because your personal values must harmonize with those of the organization you work for; otherwise, you'll experience unnecessary cognitive dissonance and stress. A red flag for me that someone is out of alignment with the organization they work for is when they say, "I'm just biding my time to get to retirement." Usually that timeline is eight or nine years. To be fair, perhaps their top value is supporting their family and they see no other way to do so. I'm certain there's more to the story than financial security. Discomfort is often a sign that you need to see yourself in a new way instead of settling for the comfort zone. In the end, it's more responsible to create a wonderful life at work rather than "bide time" in hell and stay silent. When we believe we are capable of so much more, we don't have to bide time for eight years—we make change happen and stop avoiding so that we can lead our own lives as well.

Step 4: Create a New Future Self

The key to creating a new identity is to stop living from your memories of the past and start living from the vision of your future. Picture yourself as that person, and then when you come up against some sort of inner conflict, ask yourself this: If I were my future self and were fully confident and competent, I would _____. This is then what you decide to do instead of your usual pattern of avoiding, aggression, or appeasing.

My work here is influenced by Dr. Benjamin Hardy and his book *Personality Isn't Permanent*. His work confirmed what I had been practicing in my own life and with my clients for years: we all have choices about who we want to be and what we wish to co-create; we just need a path to get there. There are many techniques, but a technique I want to share is using journaling to create a new vision. Get some prompts ready before you begin journaling because once you begin journaling, if you can get into flow, it will take on a life of its own and it will feel really good. The prework is this: Who would you be when conflict arises? How would you deal with discomfort? What does your leadership look like and feel like? How do others see you? What do people say about you? How do you define yourself? Next, make a list of positive emotions you want to feel. Here are some to start with: excited, joyful, relieved, proud, open, grateful, satisfied, engaged, engrossed, interested. Now that you have this list of emotive words top of mind, grab a journal. Pretend you're writing to an old friend you haven't seen in a decade. Describe your life and your journey as if it's already happened using the emotive language to feel your way into this new visualized reality you're creating.

SAMPLE WRITING

Dear Jane,

I can't tell you how wonderful my work is at Acme Corporation. Two years ago, I got the promotion I'd been working for, and I've learned so much about myself and my ability to create collaboration. I'm so grateful for my team, who brings their talents to work every day. We have a lot of fun, and we even got through the merger with a lot of integrity and new insights. Every day I wake up with a new sense of purpose and interest. My executive leader has given me a lot of encouragement about taking on another exciting project, and I'm anticipating the possibility of another advancement.

Your letter should be at least five times longer than this one because you want time to get into the flow. This isn't a checklist; it's an experience. You need time to relax into it until your pen is moving and the thoughts are flowing through you. This should be done with a pen and paper instead of on a computer, but this gives you an idea. Perhaps this feels a bit mystical or touchy-feely. Try not to judge it. Just do it and see what happens. When you merge emotion with fantasy, your brain starts to create new connections that make it easier for you to step into the new reality. I call it "laying tracks." If you want a new leadership identity, you have to see it and feel it first.

Step 5: Build Self-Trust

Then it's about trying on new behaviors one at a time until you create a strong sense of trust in yourself. Self-trust occurs when you say you're going to do something and then you do it. It's not rocket science. The best way to see evidence that you're changing is to do what you say you're going to do and watch the results. Notice how you feel more confident. Notice that what was scary three months ago is now becoming fun and then finally a new habit. Trying to hammer out new behaviors when every bone in your body rejects the behaviors is a tough way to arrive. Laying some tracks makes trying on the behaviors a little easier.

Skills Practice

When talking about yourself in the future, say, "I am the kind of person who is willing to be uncomfortable in order to grow, and I'm not the type to avoid conflict." Leadership is not a role or a title; it's a state of being and a way of behaving. When you get distracted by game playing, toxicity, fear of not being liked, and office politics, you lose focus. You need to strengthen your leadership identity. When it comes to creating a new identity, you don't have to guess like you do in a game of paper, scissors, rock, where paper covers rock, rock crushes scissors, and scissors cuts paper. Leadership always wins. Leadership trumps bullying. Leadership trumps drama. Leadership trumps avoidance. Leadership trumps nice. You don't have to memorize scripts or a bunch of rules. You are leadership. You live it and you breathe it. You face conflict head on. You are no longer guided by the identity of being too nice, or hands off, or best friends. Principles and values guide your decision-making, and your decisions are aligned with the values of your organization.

Reflection

1. What is your leadership identity?

2. What has leadership taught you so far?

3. How do you describe yourself?

4. Describe how your future self is different from your current self.

3

Leadership Clarity:
Staying the Course

*Leadership identity is about how
you see yourself, and leadership clarity is
about how you see the situation.*

Several years ago, I was part of a peer group for the purpose of business growth and collaboration, where one member, Barbara, constantly caused disruption. She seemed to disagree with just about every idea. If someone suggested going to dinner at seven, she thought seven-thirty was better. Barbara always had a better idea, a better way to say something, or a better understanding of a subject than you did. Barbara constantly interrupted to correct someone's grammar or share her two cents about trivial issues, and the few times anyone pushed back, she felt "misunderstood." Even though every one of us in this group could be considered a leader, we lacked leadership clarity.

In this chapter, we'll look at the three components that make up leadership clarity and what distinguishes leadership identity from leadership clarity. I'll show you how to identify obstacles and distractions so that you make better decisions from the start, and I'll give you a "leadership clarity formula" to use before you start problem-solving. Toward the end, I'll share some skills and techniques you can put into practice immediately to increase your leadership clarity for the purpose of resolving conflict.

When we think of conflict, we often think of the boss-employee conflict, and we forget that even high-level leaders, including boards of directors, executive committees, and peer groups, can also experience high conflict. Sometimes group conflict arises due to personalities and perspectives that emerge during group dynamics of forming, storming, norming, and performing. At other times, there's a lack of connection or too many diverse opinions about the purpose of the group.

The peer group I was in started out strong in the forming stage, but we had lost connection and focus. We couldn't seem to get past the storming stage. Our group was experiencing conflict, even though we might not have categorized it that way. On a more personal level, I noticed my internal conflict, and that's always a sign that there's an elephant in the room. Was the issue group dynamics, or was the issue Barbara?

I had a unique opportunity to observe Barbara outside of our immediate group. At a conference Barbara and I happened to be attending, I invited her to join me and a colleague, Rena, for lunch. I watched Barbara give sophomoric advice to Rena about how to get an organization to hand over their client list. Not only did Barbara misunderstand the context of Rena's business problem, she also didn't realize that you can't just ask a client for their marketing list. I felt embarrassed watching Barbara admonish Rena by telling her that she needed to "stop being so resistant to good advice." Rena simply listened, occasionally glancing at me and cutting her eyes to signify she had tuned out. Perhaps the real value here was seeing how easily Barbara took center stage doling out advice and what she considered to be superior business expertise when she didn't understand the complexities in the first place. The same things were happening in our peer group, but no one seemed to want to challenge Barbara's strong opinions.

Well, let me back up. Paul, a member of our group, often went toe to toe, but most of the interactions were disruptive and non-productive. Paul's aggressiveness didn't change Barbara's behavior, and the ones who truly suffered from the negativity kept quiet. Looking back, I see that none of us, including myself, had the capacity for handling Barbara. I thought about something I've said many times: the one with clarity navigates the ship. Was Barbara the one who had the most clarity? After all, she seemed to be navigating the ship.

Yes, Barbara had clarity—about her own goals, wishes, and desires—and Barbara had a strong will, just like some of the employees or colleagues you work with, I'm sure. Some might classify Barbara as high conflict or high maintenance. Barbara had a strong personality, and she was outspoken and opinionated. She had a strong sense of leadership identity, but her clarity was self-centered on her own agenda, not aligned with group goals. If Barbara was operating from *leadership clarity*, she would have been more aware of group dynamics, and her behaviors would have aligned with our stated purpose. Without a designated captain, the one with the strongest agenda, personality, or will navigates the ship.

Barbara was just being Barbara, and no one had enough clarity to seek group alignment. Barbara's actions encapsulate the idea of people doing what they do because it works. Barbara's behaviors worked for her, just not for anyone else or for the betterment of the group. Does this sound like anyone you know? Maybe a strong-minded employee with a lot of blind spots who means well but rubs other employees the wrong way? If you have a lot of internal drama and conflict, or if employees come to you complaining about a high-conflict person, be careful how you handle the situation. It's tempting to move the problem employee to another location, change shifts, or try to manipulate the situation by appeasing.

Instead, what you need is the clarity to make aligned decisions—leadership clarity.

— Leadership Clarity versus Leadership Identity —

So, how is leadership clarity distinct from leadership identity? Leadership identity is about how you see yourself, and *leadership clarity is how you see the situation.* Leadership identity is about the inner game of seeing yourself as a leader and about responsibility for the energy you bring to any situation. If you don't identify as a leader, you won't take ownership. You wait for direction. In contrast, leadership clarity is knowing what outcome you want and aligning that outcome to an agreed-upon purpose and core values. The outer game of leadership clarity is the act of speaking to the vision instead of to the problem.

Without a strong sense of leadership clarity, it's easy to overreact to internal conflicts, avoiding the situation entirely or smoothing things over in order to feel better. So, what about simply leaving a group? Isn't that leadership clarity in action? Leaving a dysfunctional group might possibly be based on leadership clarity, but a better example of leadership clarity is to become captain of the ship instead of being swayed by every rough wind.

What's interesting is that in our professional group, each one of us identified as being a leader, yet we struggled with leadership clarity. With enough leadership clarity, any one of us could have easily course corrected. Instead, we focused on what we perceived to be an obstacle: Barbara. There are a dozen strategies we could have applied, some of which will be introduced in this book. *What we often forget is that even if we aren't formally in charge, we don't necessarily have to sit back and allow the ship to veer off course.* We almost always have at least a few choices available to us. We don't always have to wait for an authority figure to right the ship. As leaders, if we can build leadership clarity, we will take aligned action to resolve virtually any conflict.

It's a common mistake to get distracted by focusing on what everyone else is doing wrong. Leadership clarity is about declaring the desired outcome while seeing the entire situation for what it is and using leadership skills to refocus energy. Revisiting my definition for leadership: if leadership is about anything, it is about alignment, and alignment is about focusing energy. Instead of looking at obstacles, leadership clarity puts focus on the outcomes and on supporting others to achieve higher business goals. Gaining clarity about the desired outcome would have prevented side conversations, getting distracted, and letting the elephant stay in the room for so long. Leadership clarity is about making decisions based on values and outcomes.

Feeling Your Way to Clarity

A good way to tell that you need to focus on leadership clarity is by noticing your thoughts and feelings. If you start feeling unsafe, aggressive, unhappy, or stressed, it probably means there's some sort of inner conflict brewing that points to an outer conflict that's going to emerge. I'm not saying that feelings are right or wrong. I'm saying that your emotional energy is telling you to get curious and to take measures to seek understanding. The first part of your focus has to be inward; otherwise, you'll blame "Barbara" and not be any better off than you were. Look inward first. When you're aligned with values and stated objectives, you make good decisions. When you focus on the problem being outside of yourself, you don't.

I didn't like my thoughts about Barbara, and I noticed that I started to focus more on Barbara than our shared purpose for coming together in the first place. Others seemed to do the same. Even though this group was what I would call *high integrity*, occasionally we engaged in side conversations about Barbara's rude behavior. I'd be misrepresenting myself if I didn't admit how delighted I was to get social proof that "it's not just me" who felt that way. If you notice yourself gossiping or gathering social proof, it's a sign you need to step away and exercise some leadership clarity.

Three Questions

When you find yourself complaining, distracted, or unhappy, the very first question you need to ask is, *What do I want?* If you can answer that question, you can get immediate clarity. What's interesting is that most people can't answer the "What do I want?" question. Most of us talk about the problem, and we get distracted by the circumstance, distracted by what others think, or in this case, distracted by some other person's behavior.

Once you answer the question "What do I want?" ask yourself a second question: "How does this desire align with my values and the values of the organization?" For example, if fairness is a top value, then you have to say, "Is what I want an example of fairness, or is it one sided?" Then you have to ask the third question. The third question is, "What would this (thing I want) give me that I don't have now?" The reason I give you this third question is to make sure you're telling yourself the truth about what you want instead of trying to problem-solve. If you say something like, "I want Barbara to leave this group," then you're speaking to the problem, and problem-solving. You believe that the only reason you aren't being productive is due to Barbara. When you reflect and ask, "Is this fair?" you'd have to say, "Not without talking with Barbara and giving her a chance." Then going one step further, you ask yourself, "What would removing Barbara give me that I don't have now?" You might say, "I'd feel more respect, and the group would be more positive." Now you've gotten to the root of what you want. You want more mutual respect and a more positive, supportive experience. I can almost hear the debate: "But removing Barbara would give me what I want, so what's wrong with that?" Removing Barbara might give you the experience you want, but removing Barbara before addressing the problem won't help you grow as a leader, and it wouldn't be fair to Barbara, to the group, nor to your own desire for growth. Getting clear about the end result in spite of Barbara will improve your leadership and help you build courage.

These same principles apply when you have an annoying employee. Don't move the employee out of the department, where someone else in your organization inherits the same problem. Stop avoiding and start leading. Here's an exercise to keep you honest. Take a moment to answer these simple questions.

───────────────── Exercise ─────────────────

- ➡ What conflict are you currently having?
- ➡ What are you thinking?
- ➡ What are you feeling?
- ➡ Who is involved?
- ➡ How long has this been going on?

Now that you've answered these questions, answer this one: What have you tried so far to correct the situation? Nothing yet, you say? Haven't had time? You already know what they'll say? Tell the truth here: Have you been avoiding the problem? If so, why? Do you believe it's an inner-game issue or an outer-game issue, or both? Would your company culture support your intervention if you tried? These questions aren't to make you feel bad but to help you discern what's really going on. You probably have good reasons for not addressing the problem. Perhaps you fear that your employer wouldn't support you, or you have evidence that the other person will be very defensive—you've seen it before. Maybe you know deep down that you need to develop some serious skills, and that's why you're reading this book. These are valid observations. Stay with me and we will talk about resistance training in chapter 6, and then you'll see what to do and how to lead even when there's extreme resistance from the other person.

To gain clarity, we have to first admit how often we mismanage conflict and what methods we use to avoid. We appease and say things we don't agree with, and we try to win someone over at the expense of our own values. Or we get aggressive and try to show some teeth, thus avoiding an honest conversation that seems risky. Then there's just good old avoidance in the purest form where we decide to remove ourselves from the situation completely or ride it out until we have completed our commitments.

One reason you feel nervous about bringing the elephant into the room is that unresolved or mismanaged conflict creates uncertainty. You aren't after certainty here, and I would be remiss if I didn't make a distinction between clarity and certainty. Clarity is not certainty. Clarity is a feeling of peace, where you've weighed the situation, you know your next right step, and you're willing to accept the risk and the consequences with no hidden agenda. When it comes to relationship dynamics, there's no such thing as certainty, but you'll know clarity when you feel it. Clarity always comes before alignment. Once you're clear about your own values and you're aligned within, you must align with the values, policies, and outcomes of your organization. We'll talk more about how culture affects decision-making, but know this: your values must align with your organization's values or you'll continue to experience confusion and misalignment if you decide to stay anyway.

Inner Peace Equals Clarity

Here is a practical decision you can make, and this decision will serve you every single time you face conflict with another person: decide to always seek inner peace. *Inner peace is a good sign that you're clear.* If you experience any kind of disturbing emotions like resentment and you find yourself thinking vengeful thoughts, you aren't clear enough to make a good decision. Surely you've had the experience of telling someone off, or shot off a terse email when you were angry, only to regret it later. When your emotions are high, your decisions won't be aligned with your purpose or core values. Inner peace, also known as inner alignment, happens when you know who you are, what you want, and what it will take to align your choices with your core values. You can't make decisions you aren't willing to take responsibility for. You risk your reputation, peace of mind, and health when you make decisions that are misaligned with your values.

Once you get the inner game right, every other decision will be easier, and every skill you learn by reading this book will give you the confidence to handle conflict, initiate difficult conversations, and regulate your emotions while doing so. I'll share a personal example that has served me well. I decided that I would never agree to do anything that might make me feel resentment or regret. Why? Because one of my guiding principles is that I'm totally responsible for my life experience. No matter how much someone says "Trust me," my goal is to trust myself. If I go along with something that doesn't seem right, or if I agree to trust someone else before trusting myself, the question I ask is, Can I do this and accept the consequences if things don't work out? This tells me whether the decision really belongs to me or if I'm trying to appease someone else before pleasing myself. This decision has never once guided me in the wrong direction. How might this decision work for you? Suppose one of your values is to fully support your own boss, but then a situation arises where some coworkers try to convince you to keep information from your boss. They say, "Trust me, it will be OK," and they say, "If anything happens, we have your back." Then when something happens, they are nowhere to be found and you end up looking deceitful. My point here is to be true to yourself. You'll never go wrong.

— Three Core Components of Leadership Clarity —

Leadership clarity has three core components: the situation, the outcome, and the obstacle. The situation is point A, the outcome is point B, and the obstacle is the barrier or barriers between point A and point B. Let's take a moment and see if you can identify the three different points of a conflict you're currently facing.

1. What's the situation?

2. What's the desired end result?

3. What are the obstacles?

To make this concept come alive with narrative, I often use a mental model that I call "the language of the island" (see figure 3).

The boat is point A, the island is point B, and the shark is the obstacle. Let's look at how point A and point B create dynamic tension and how to view obstacles that keep you stuck.

Point A is where you are now, your current situation. Point A also represents a hidden desire—a desire to grow, to change, to improve, or to experience. Where conflict or workplace drama is concerned, point A is often about a current conflict that needs

FIGURE 3. The language of the island

resolution. If point A is a toxic work environment, and the unwanted turnover is the result, your point A has woven into it a desire to get to point B, job satisfaction. If two people have filed an EEOC complaint (point A), your desire is to get to point B, where people are happy and working together again. As a leader you need the skill to adequately describe the facts of the situation without letting emotions distract you and get the best of you. It can feel pretty bad to admit the ship has veered off course and you don't know what to do. It's easy to blame a person or a group of people to alleviate the internal pressure. Don't make the common mistake of rushing to a solution before describing the situation accurately. Don't sign everyone up for a workshop, and don't start an engagement initiative. Don't move the complainers and blamers to another department to keep the peace. It's not yet time for problem-solving. And for goodness' sake, stop saying things like "We are all adults," "I shouldn't have to tell them," and "It will all blow over when Kim retires." It's time to learn how to purposefully describe the current reality and the intended outcome, and we will do that in a moment!

Point B is your outcome, or ideally a shared future vision not yet created. If your point A is about a specific conflict, point B is about resolving the conflict. The outcome is somewhere in the future, whether that future is one week, three months, or five years away. I'd be remiss if I didn't say how important a shared vision is to co-creating the outcomes you want in an organization. People support what they help to create, and they resist what they don't understand. Point B is an exciting vision that can be seen by all who are helping to create it.

You will struggle to arrive at point B if you fail to align actions with the core values of your organization or if you fail to engage others in the journey. In other words, the means to getting to your outcome must support the ends. There are all kinds of ways to get to an end result, but the way to get there using *leadership clarity* is to make sure that your actions and language are congruent with the values the company was built on if you want to maintain trust in the organization.

In my experience, most employees can't recite their company's stated values. There's often a disconnect between what is stated on the walls and what actually happens in the halls. Values live in the realm of the invisible. It takes work to make values come alive and not just act as slogans or aspirations. As a leader, you have to constantly reinforce the company's values in everything you do; otherwise, the values are of no real power. Every decision should be based on the stated values. For example, if one of your core values is collaboration, you could give awards based on collaboration, or you might recognize someone's extraordinary efforts when they collaborated. Or on the opposite side of the spectrum, if someone made a decision that wasn't for the good of the organization, you ask what they could have done to become more collaborative. When I have done workshops on values, I often ask the group to agree on what is the highest value of the organization. I asked this question once with a group of hospital executives and directors. They said their highest value was compassion. My next question was, "What does compassion look like at your hospital?" No one had an example. They hadn't really thought about the word and what it means, what it looks like in action, and what the absence of compassion looks like.

I was on a phone call with an executive who was losing a lot of new employees in the housekeeping department during their first week. This executive told me that the employees with the most seniority were bullying the new employees. I asked her what the managers were doing to stop the problem. She hadn't thought about that. I looked up their website to see that their values were dignity, respect, and compassion. What I can tell you is that if employees treat each other disrespectfully, they aren't treating their patients any better. The values were not lived in this organization, and instead of talking with the managers in charge, this executive was problem-solving by moving people around and asking me for a workshop. Values aren't a map, but more of a north star. Knowing which way is north saves a lot of time when you're managing conflict. Once you have these two points of reference and you can accurately describe point A and point B, you increase your capacity for leadership clarity, a skill that will serve you in every area of life. But there will always be obstacles and distractions between point A and point B.

Obstacles and Distractions

Obstacles materialize in many forms. An obstacle can be legislation that doesn't align with your plans. Obstacles can be about resources, finances, or expertise. Obstacles can arise as an unexpected tragedy or simply a lack of know-how. Distractions, on the other hand, get us off course without our awareness. A distraction is when you're having a difficult conversation about performance, but your employee points out that the other employees said something negative about your leadership. If you take the bait, the direction of the conversation changes without you even knowing it. Instead of going to the island called Improve Your Performance, you go to the island called Listening to Gossip. Either way, obstacles and distractions vie for attention and shift our focus. Focusing on obstacles (conflict) before focusing on outcomes will always lead to more obstacles, more distractions, and more conflict. What happens when you focus on obstacles first is that you allow yourself to be guided by the problems of the past and present instead of focusing on the promise of the new future. The obstacles will be there for sure, but first if you want to gain leadership clarity, you have to clearly articulate the two points of reference. This takes discipline and focus.

The Leadership Clarity Formula

To develop leadership clarity, you must get good at identifying and articulating point A and point B. Otherwise you'll get off track and won't know why. When enough conflict erupts, as conflict does during change, don't jump immediately into problem-solving, and don't start a new initiative before you can clearly describe the situation and your desired outcome. Seek expertise to help you work through the process if you need support, but don't tell the expert what to do. If you already knew what to do, then you wouldn't be confused. Seek out someone who can ask good questions without proposing premature solutions. When I'm getting ready to work with someone, my goal is to understand their point A and their point B and the size of the gap. Think of point A as being "Where we are now" and point B as "What I want" (see figure 4).

Leaders struggle when they try to propose a solution before adequately describing and defining point A or point B. For example, a co-owner of a small enterprise called me to talk about a problem—the current director.

"He's just dead weight to this organization," the vice president said.

FIGURE 4. Point A and point B

"What's the problem?" I asked.

"He's just not a good leader."

"What do you mean?"

"It's hard to say."

"Try," I urged him on.

"He just has an entitled mentality."

"What is he doing that he shouldn't be doing?"

"Nothing I can put my finger on."

"How is this problem affecting business outcomes?"

"Hmmm, I just think someone else could do a better job."

"What is he not doing that you need him to do?"

"He's just not a great fit for this position."

On and on the conversation went, and I had no more clarity about the situation than I did from the start. This executive was not clear about the situation or how the situation affected business outcomes.

"How long has he worked for you?" I asked.

"Well, I inherited him."

"Maybe so, but my question is how long has he worked for you?"

"Twelve years or so."

Notice the pattern here. There is dissatisfaction at point A, but the executive can't describe the situation or the intended outcome. Here is a method to get point A right. Answer the following questions:

1. What is happening that should not be happening?

2. What is not happening that should be happening?

3. How does this affect the business?

Right now, you aren't concerned with who's to blame or who's accountable. You're looking only at the *situation*: what's happening that should not be happening. There's time to add names later. The reason we aren't concerned with names in the beginning is because you don't want to get distracted by blame. You want to understand the problem from a business perspective. When you get frustrated, it's easy to start blaming and making assumptions. There's an inner game at stake here: keeping the emotions regulated so you can clearly describe what's happening or not happening without getting triggered into high conflict before having all the facts. You want to be dispassionate in looking at the evidence and facts of point A. After we get the situation nailed down, we can look at who's involved for the purpose of correcting performance or understanding the individual's point of view, but at the beginning we're not concerned with who, just what.

Example 1

The documents are getting turned in on Thursday, and they should be getting turned in on Tuesdays. This affects our ability to meet payroll on time. One of our core values is punctuality, and this problem is not aligned with that value.

Notice in this example, I was able to reinforce the issue by stating the core values. You may not always be able to do this, but it's often a helpful reinforcement.

Example 2

The air temperature has not been regulated the last week. The air temperature is eighty-six degrees and should be sixty-eight degrees. This problem creates product waste and is costing materials loss and labor for rework. One of our core values is quality, and we are not meeting standards.

Before you ever talk to anyone about the problem, you should be able to dispassionately describe the situation and how the situation affects the business outcomes. In this example, I reinforced the need for change by addressing misalignment with a core value of quality. Point B, your outcome, is somewhere in the future, whether that future is within one week, three months, or five years. The invisible elements of mission, vision, and values are there to help you know if you're heading north instead of south. Most of us don't really understand how to use the power of these invisible forces because we aren't in the habit of *living our values* or making decisions in alignment with values. Regarding the group where we struggled with Barbara, someone could have said, "Are we really supporting each other right now? Or have we lost focus?" Vision, mission, and values are markers we can use to realign if we have a clearly defined and agreed-upon picture of point B.

Practical Tools and Techniques

Now that you understand the principles of leadership clarity, let's look at some outer-game skills you can use when you're in small conflicts like the one where Barbara was viewed as an obstacle.

Skill 1: Represent Yourself

It's tempting to start talking about how everyone feels, but this is a bad strategy that causes hurt feelings. To ensure success, make it a rule to simply represent yourself. For example, if Barbara keeps interrupting everyone, you don't say to Barbara, "Everyone is really tired of you interrupting." Instead, just represent yourself and say, "Barbara, I want you to let me finish speaking," or "Barbara, when you interrupt Janet, it throws me off. I'd like to hear Janet's points before we start offering advice." You can even say something to a very small group like, "I know we all want to support each other, but I'm sensing a negative vibe, and I'd like to reset the room by stating our purpose."

When you represent yourself, you aren't representing a group, or a culture, or any other entity. You aren't saying "as a woman," or "on behalf of all leaders," or "as a minority," or "as part of the LGBT community." You aren't trying to take on the world's social issues. When you represent yourself, you're talking about *your* experience, *your* perspective, and *your* feelings, which cannot be debated or denied.

With that said, in certain circumstances, you may indeed choose to speak for the group, or you may need to speak for the group—for example, if you clearly see examples of social injustice, sexism, prejudice, violence, or wrongs against humanity—but here we're simply talking about your own issues that can be solved by representing yourself, instead of taking on the world's issues. If you do choose to represent a group, be conscious about your tone, intention, and approach, and make sure the group backs you up. I've spoken up for a group before and had the group not back me up when all was said and done. I find it more empowering to represent myself.

You also take a risk when you represent yourself because others may say, "I don't feel that way at all," or "You're a bit sensitive, aren't you?" Don't let those kinds of comments distract you or bait you for an argument about reality. Simply say, "That's fine," or "I hear you. I'm simply stating what's true for me and asking for what I want." You don't necessarily need to get agreement; you just need the courage to take responsibility for your own experience.

With that said, ask yourself what outcome you seek by representing yourself. If you don't know what you want, then your criticism may come off as a complaint. Be ready to ask for what you want to make things right, rather than trying to "be right" by making everyone else wrong. If you don't yet know what would fix the situation, you may need to schedule a private conversation and do some preparation before your conversation. Don't act only from emotion.

There's a lot of unresolved conflict in the world, and we're in the process of learning the best approaches to overcome our inner and outer conflicts to get the outcomes we want. My best advice is don't react to triggers from high emotion or unhealed wounds. Process emotions first to gain clarity on what you really want. We'll talk more about the use of emotions in the next chapter. Use discernment and ask yourself if this is the time and place to speak up and if you can do so with emotional integrity to achieve a positive outcome.

Skill 2: Speak to the Vision

Often, you'll find yourself in a conversation where the conversation is about the obstacles. Or you notice the conversation becoming disruptive. This is your opportunity to speak to the vision. Even when the discussion is getting heated, you can say something like, "Look, it seems that we are both passionate about our point of view and we disagree. I know this is uncomfortable, but we don't have to be here tomorrow or in a week. What I want is . . ." Then you simply speak to the future you want. "I want us to help each other achieve our goals. This time next year we will have so many things to celebrate."

If you've ever had a conversation go south when you thought you were clear, chances are either you or someone else had some hidden intentions or unresolved emotions you were unaware of. Misunderstandings and hurt feelings happen in one-on-one conversations, team meetings, Zoom trainings, and large events. When you lead, prepare to be caught off guard and misunderstood. Your well-prepared conversation can be disrupted by distractions even when in a group setting. Always strive to create leadership clarity. Practice emotional awareness. Anticipate obstacles. Prepare yourself with skills. Have an alternate plan ready so that you maintain composure and focus and don't default to defensiveness.

Reflection

1. Describe an unresolved conflict.

2. Describe an outcome you would like to achieve.

3. What obstacle seems to be in your way?

4. What have you tried to do to address the conflict?

5. What tools in this chapter can help you address conflict differently?

4

Emotional Integrity:
Anger Is Not the Truth

*Think of blame as a shortcut
for avoiding responsibility.*

Jack, an energetic self-proclaimed business geek, started working as a business manager in the family construction business his father, Leroy, had started over thirty years ago. Jack had never been close to his father, but a decade after getting his business degree, and with a hunger to learn, Jack saw an opportunity to help his father make the business profitable again.

Jack saw dozens of ways to cut costs, improve production, and save time. Jack's enthusiasm, knack for numbers, and loyalty to his dad seemed like a recipe for success, but instead, Leroy took Jack's ideas as criticism or as one-upmanship. When Jack tried to implement a new software program or present a standard operating procedure, Leroy would say, "That's not the way we do things around here. I'm not gonna fix it if it ain't broken."

The business hadn't turned a profit in three years. Leroy just refused to acknowledge the truth. No matter how Jack tried to help, Leroy knew better, found fault, and criticized Jack. "You think you know more than me? I've worked in construction longer than you've been alive," he would say. Leroy's temperament was difficult for Jack to understand, much less tolerate. Leroy took his frustrations out on Jack, slamming doors, cursing, and throwing tools. He was unstable, unpredictable, and volatile. On the few occasions Jack tried to calm his father, Leroy didn't take responsibility for his emotional outbursts. Instead, he blamed Jack, and all too often Jack compensated by walking on eggshells, trying to off-site when his dad got to the office, hiding information, and apologizing for things he wasn't responsible for.

Not only was Jack's father failing as a role model and a leader, he was losing the inner game.

Who do you relate to more? Leroy or Jack? To be transparent, I can identify with both Jack and Leroy on some level. I've had plenty of instances where I blamed someone else for my experience, and I've lost my temper a time or two . . . well, maybe dozens of times. I've also walked on eggshells or overcompensated for some pretty dysfunctional relationships that I tried to fix but couldn't.

Strong emotions have the capacity to derail any one of us, given the right timing and circumstances. The bigger problem is when we have no control and are at the mercy of our triggers or how we feel on any given day. In this chapter we'll look at how strong emotions hijack our decision-making abilities and why self-regulation is the key to maintaining balance. We'll look at how the brain works when we're angry, and I'll give some tips to help you start the rewiring process to emotional integrity.

If we're honest with ourselves, we all have a little of Jack and a little of Leroy inside of us. It's difficult to change ingrained patterns. Whatever you do over and over again builds neuro-connections in the brain that become habits. When you succumb to your impulses and feelings, you lose the inner game and become weaker with each avoidance. Every time you betray yourself to take on someone else's emotional well-being, you're unconsciously buying into an idea that they will change, when in fact they don't see any reason to change.

In order to change, you need to increase self-awareness, but self-awareness without the skill set of self-regulation will not help you to actually change your patterns. I've known plenty of self-aware people who can't seem to shift their unwanted behavioral patterns even though they want to. What's needed is not only emotional intelligence but emotional integrity.

The term "emotional integrity" has been introduced by others but isn't a commonly used term. I'd like to bring the term emotional integrity into our common language and make some distinctions between emotional awareness, emotional intelligence, and emotional integrity. Emotional awareness is a prerequisite for building *emotional intelligence*, and emotional intelligence is essential for building emotional integrity. Let's break it down. Emotional awareness is being aware of how emotional energy processes through your body. Emotional intelligence is the capacity to be aware of, control, and express one's emotions and to handle interpersonal relationships judiciously and empathetically. What makes emotional integrity distinct is the commitment to let others know about what's going on inside of you before you lash out or withdraw, and the willingness to circle back around to finish a conversation you needed to withdraw from.

—— Three Components of Emotional Integrity ——

Emotional integrity doesn't mean being perfect, achieving complete stability, avoiding anger, or staying quiet to keep peace. Emotional integrity requires three courageous components:

1. The courage to take responsibility for your experience

2. The ability to face your dark side

3. The willingness to represent yourself

First, the courage to take responsibility for your experience: this means no blaming others for your feelings and reactions, even if they did something wrong. Second, the ability to face your dark side: this means telling the truth to yourself about your jealousy, anger, resentment, and unresolved issues. Third, the willingness to represent yourself: this means letting others know what's going on inside of you, whether that's a story you're telling yourself or a feeling that you can't seem to stop.

Representing yourself keeps you honest with others. There's no more hiding. Believe me when I say that these three components keep you honest. The end game here is self-awareness and self-regulation. It is difficult to shift your patterns without these three components simply because we human beings justify our behaviors, and we even lie to ourselves about what we really feel because we fear judgment. When you openly admit what you're thinking or feeling to another person, it changes the game.

It's OK to say, "I'm in a bad mood and can't do small talk right now." It's OK to say, "I need some space because I'm struggling to maintain my composure." It's OK to say, "I am boiling with rage and need to release some energy before I come back to this project." It's OK to say, "The story I'm telling myself is that you really aren't interested." Most of the time we let our energy escape, and eventually someone we care about becomes the unfortunate target no matter how self-aware we are. If this happens to you, and you often feel regret over your own behavior, this chapter will help you make sense of what's going on, and you can forgive yourself and rewire your brain to align with the real you—not the angry, unreasonable you.

It's especially important to develop emotional integrity as a leader. If you want to attract high-level employees, you can't be known for throwing temper tantrums, being erratic, or failing to self-regulate. These patterns only show emotional immaturity and a lack of self-awareness, not leadership. It's also important to develop emotional integrity as an employee, a colleague, a parent, a sibling, and a friend if you want to build trusting relationships. Relationships built on trust offer a solid foundation for life enjoyment and personal growth, while relationships built on manipulation and dysfunction contribute to all kinds of life problems, including health issues over time.

Whether your habit is lashing out, as Leroy did, or taking on issues that don't belong to you, as Jack did, you have to build new pathways, and it's difficult. But once you've shifted a pattern three times, the pathways start to get stronger! If you mismanage conflict by avoiding or losing control, what kind of role model are you for others? Here are some practices and steps I've used successfully with myself and many of my clients to become better at self-regulation. Self-regulation is essential to achieving emotional integrity because if you can't self-regulate, you won't be able to achieve the three core components. Instead, you'll buy into your anger, and you'll feel justified at your outbursts only to feel shame later and repeat the patterns again. I can't say it enough: self-regulation is key to achieving emotional integrity and staying out of regret. The way you take responsibility for your feelings is to take responsibility for your own self-regulation.

— Self-Regulation and Cognitive Restructuring —

You're not at the mercy of your emotions, thoughts, and feelings. There are ways to restructure your brain, and it's called cognitive restructuring! If you're the type of person who is passionate, feels intense anger, and then acts swiftly, only to have regrets later, it doesn't mean you're a bad person or that you can never change. Instead, it means that you don't know how anger works in your brain, and when you get extremely angry, it feels like it's important to take immediate action. So, you go ahead and tell someone off or make a rash decision to end a relationship without understanding the whole story. That's because the part of your brain that can make good decisions is overtaken by another part of your brain that wants to survive. Your anger made you believe that your perceptions were "the truth." You didn't have the ability to doubt your bias and assumptions because the emotion was so strong it convinced you to act. I like to think of anger as energy that wants to go somewhere, and that's why we lash out—to release the energy.

Even though I'm not a neuroscientist, I want to offer a basic understanding of how your brain works when triggered and how you can use this knowledge to stay in control. Here's how it works. Your brain has a section that controls emotion, mood, and basic survival functions. It's called the limbic system. Inside the limbic system is a structure called the amygdala. When the amygdala gets triggered, it completely takes over the part of your brain that controls your executive function, the part that helps you make good decisions based on fact. That's because the amygdala is in the subconscious mind and works only on behalf of your survival. The amygdala isn't concerned with logic, only emotions.

Then there's the executive function of your brain, called the prefrontal cortex. The prefrontal cortex controls the conscious mind, and it's your conscious mind that helps you make good decisions and think about the bigger picture. When you get extremely angry, you lose executive function and thus the capability of making grounded decisions.

The stronger your prefrontal cortex, the more agency you create in your own life and the more control you have over directing your subconscious mind so that the amygdala stays calm and doesn't cause disruption. Therefore, building emotional integrity requires that you build up your prefrontal cortex, the decision-making part of your brain, so that you aren't the victim of your subconscious programming and triggers. The problem is, we want so much to trust our feelings. What do feelings really mean?

What Feelings Mean

We always look for signs to tell us if we're going in the right direction or not. We say things like, "I just have a feeling about this," and "Trust your gut, it's never wrong." We get opinions from our colleagues and friends before making important decisions because we need to "feel good" about our decisions. We listen for something soothing so that we'll finally know the right answer when faced with uncertainty. The question is, How do you know for sure your gut isn't wrong? When do you need to trust your feelings, and when do you need to do a little more research?

Feelings (the way you interpret emotions) are there for a reason, but we need to use discernment when we interpret what they mean; otherwise, our interpretations work against us. What does anger mean to you? Does it mean that someone did you wrong, or does it mean that you don't fully understand what's going on and you need further investigation? *My clients find it helpful to change their interpretation of anger as a sign that they need to act, but they also need more information so they can take the right action.* When we interpret our anger as justification for lashing out, we usually have regrets later.

Here's a quick quiz: Suppose you're running late and sitting in traffic. The light has turned green, but the person in front of you seems preoccupied and doesn't move. You honk your horn a friendly little toot-toot to get their attention, but nothing happens. You scream out loud, "How much greener does it need to be to get you to move?!" Nothing happens, and you're fuming. Now you have to sit through another red light. You look for another lane to get into and nothing opens, but then, you hear a siren. The ambulance is coming toward the car in front of you. You find out that the person in the car ahead of you was suffering a medical emergency. Now you have new meaning about why they sat through the light and why your honking didn't do any good. *The situation is the same, but your understanding of it changed.* Now you aren't so worried about being late. You're more concerned that the person in front of you gets medical attention, and you say a quick prayer of gratitude for your health.

Good decision-making requires steady emotions and a peaceful mind. To be good at conflict management, leaders need to be good decision-makers. Unprocessed emotions impede good decision-making and create barriers to managing conflict effectively. If your interpretation of anger is that you're the only one who's right in a given situation, that interpretation is going to cause unnecessary conflict.

Perhaps if Leroy or Jack would have set clear expectations of how to work together, and if they could have done some strategic planning and made some initial agreement, there wouldn't be so much anger and so many unmet or unrealistic expectations on both sides.

Feelings can be a guidepost or lead you astray depending on how you interpret your feelings. Even when you really want to change, it can seem so difficult. One tool you can use to change your wiring is learning how to work with your narrative.

——— Take Responsibility for Your Narrative ———

We human beings are similar in our makeup. We have a thought, and that thought turns into an interpretation. The interpretation turns into a narrative, or a story, if you will, and then we believe the story we've told ourselves about what happened, who's at fault, and what their intention was. All we do is perceive and assume. We have to make judgments to live, but if you believe everything you think, you'll be at the mercy of your beliefs and you'll never question their validity. We all have a little voice inside our head telling us how things are, and we create our own reality, whether we're aware of it or not.

Another part of our brain, called the reticular activating system, is always looking for evidence of what we already believe to be true. We get what we look for. The question is not, Do I have confirmation bias? The answer to that is yes, we all do. The point is, if you look for trouble, you'll find it. If you look for opportunity, it's always there. What we believe to be true without question will rule our lives. The real question is, How can I become aware of my confirmation bias and open myself to new possibilities? The great news is that we have the power to shift our focus and intentionally create new narratives!

I learned something fascinating when I was studying narrative coaching: our stories (narratives) are the source of our suffering. If that is true, then our stories can also be the source of our awakening. Our stories either trigger the amygdala or help us maintain self-regulation. The fact is, you can't make decisions when you're unregulated, and you can't even be coached when you're overly emotional. But through observing your emotions and the stories that trigger them, you can start building new intentional narratives.

You can't change history. For example, I can't change the fact that I started my career late in life or that I spent twenty-one years as a blue-collar factory worker. What I can change is my interpretation of what that means. You can't change the fact that you got fired, got overlooked, or suffered by someone else's poor judgment, but you can change the meaning you give to it. You can tell a story of suffering, or you can tell a story of success.

What happened, happened, but you can change the meaning about your story. As an exercise, try this week to simply become aware of interpretations and remind yourself that these are just thoughts. When in a heated moment, use this mantra: "It's not an emergency right now." If you aren't self-regulated and your mind is running wild with unfortunate scenarios, find a way to calm down and rest before approaching difficult conversations. Every bone in your body may want to lash out, but you know you aren't self-regulated when you're feeling enraged. Remember this: anger is not the truth, but it is the fuel to get you there.

This sounds easy on paper and in the workshop, but it takes courage, dedication, discipline, and practice to build emotional integrity, and here's a snapshot of how changing your patterns works in real life.

Gaining Emotional Regulation

Victor hired me to help him gain some control working with a high-conflict individual, Bill, an investor in his company. Victor wanted to manage his reactions toward Bill, who constantly corrected him and interfered in areas that didn't need his expertise. Victor and Bill usually got into heated arguments that disrupted meetings and created internal dysfunction, slowing decision-making and contributing to a negative vibe. Victor knew that learning some different skills would be invaluable to scaling his business and working with employees, investors, board members, and even Bill. One day on a call, Victor said, "I had two successes today. I didn't get triggered by a nasty email that was accusing me of doing something underhanded, and I also didn't respond immediately at a board meeting." "How did it feel?" I asked Victor. "It was so hard. It took every bone in my body not to immediately react, but I remember you saying not to give it so much energy and to buy some time. I decided to wait, knowing I had time later to address the issue when I felt more centered, and I was surprised at what happened: someone else responded to the email and told Bill he was being ridiculous. The same thing happened at the meeting!" This board had a habit of being yes-men to Bill, a highly successful businessman with a strong personality. In the past when conflict happened between Bill and Victor, everyone seemed to stay disengaged and neutral, but when Victor allowed some space, others stepped up.

A big ah-ha for Victor was the understanding that when you constantly do the emotional work of the group, you unintentionally "rip off" others from taking equal ownership. If you do all the dirty work, others will gladly disassociate, and you won't get the group engagement.

I can hear the question "But isn't staying silent avoiding?" It depends. If you're staying silent because you're afraid, then yes, it's probably avoidance. But if you consciously decide to stay silent and it's an intentional method to see where things go, then no, it's becoming more strategic in your communication and using the executive function in your brain to maintain control. Staying silent is a great strategy for creating a safe space for engagement.

Lashing out should never be plan A. What we often forget is that most of the time, there's an opportunity to circle back around to fully address the situation once we have engaged our thinking brain (the prefrontal cortex) to make a good decision about the approach. You don't have to immediately give into your urges to tell someone off, prove a point, or correct them.

We all need a variety of tools. As I told Victor, "If you already have a hammer, you don't necessarily use a hammer every single time. Sometimes you need some WD-40." Emotional integrity doesn't mean doing someone else's emotional work or always being the one to solve the problem, especially if you're a leader or working as a team or group as Victor and his board were. You can't make yourself 100 percent responsible for someone else's experience or behavior. What you can do is become a mirror of emotional integrity for them, set appropriate boundaries, and make appropriate choices. Now I'd like to give you some real exercises you can apply to let the restructuring begin!

Step 1: Stand on the Bridge and Watch the Movie

When strong emotions wash over you, it's as if you're in a rowboat on a raging river. When you feel the first wave, visualize yourself getting off the boat to go stand on the bridge. Emotional integrity requires you to become the witness and observe behaviors you exhibit when you feel threatened or experience a loss of control. Once you position yourself to stand above it all, you gain a little more control. You can watch it all play out. Pick two weeks where you observe yourself to increase awareness when you aren't in the midst of chaos. All you're doing is watching yourself. It's as if you're sitting in a movie theater watching a screen where you're the lead. You'll see drama. You'll see humor. You might be embarrassed or feel empathy. Don't hide your eyes when it gets scary. Go ahead and cry if you feel like it. Enjoy the show.

QUESTIONS TO ANSWER

1. What is the behavior you exhibit when emotions take over?

2. Why do you want to change the behavior?

3. What is the result of behaving in this dysfunctional manner?

For example, you might say, "I slam the door when I'm angry, and then I don't speak for several days. I want to change the behavior because it's making me look like a weak leader and because I want to stay with difficult conversations instead of putting up a wall. The result is that my employees walk on eggshells and avoid me, even when there's important information I need to know."

Step 2: Feel, Don't Act

Whatever triggers you creates a sensation in your body right before you act out. What triggers me might not bother you in the least. I grew up in a dysfunctional household where there was a lot of anger. To this day I still jump out of my chair when I hear a door slam or any unexpected loud noise. Don't judge your trigger, just name it. It could be technology glitches, sarcasm, traffic, or deadlines. Pay attention to what sends you to the moon, and you'll find your trigger. Your trigger produces sensations in your body—try to notice when this happens.

Notice your body's reaction, like right before you act out your coping behavior. Does your neck get hot? Do your palms sweat, or does your heart rate increase? Notice how energy processes through your body the next time you feel something you don't like.

Feeling what you feel without acting out is hard work that takes honesty and courage, and here's why: even though you're getting in touch with what you feel, you don't allow instant relief by reacting the same old way you usually do. Think of your reactions as addictive urges to release energy. There's an urge that comes with strong energy—the urge is to either avoid feeling the feeling or quickly release the energy. So, if you normally raise your voice, you control the urge to raise your voice. If you get an email that ticks you off, avoid the urge to get it off your plate and respond in all caps. Instead, acknowledge the email and let them know your response is forthcoming tomorrow. Put it on your calendar and see how different you feel after you have processed it. I know . . . it feels so good in the moment to prove them wrong, or put them in their place, but the truth is, it's not helping you in any way, shape, or form. *It only feels good now.* If you act out, you won't respect yourself in the morning. Wait until you're more centered. I know, you're dying to address the issue. Hang tight. You usually don't need to address something this red-hot minute. There's time to circle back later—trust me and trust yourself. Don't lash out, gossip, or bad-mouth other people who you think made you feel all the bad feelings you feel. You don't need to go shopping, gambling, or drinking to soothe the feelings. Learn how to let the emotional energy go through your body.

QUESTIONS TO ANSWER

1. What is one feeling you want to avoid?

2. What is your normal coping behavior?

3. What bodily sensations do you experience?

There's one problem that can happen with waiting until you calm down. Once you're calmed down, you'll want to brush over it or avoid because you no longer feel the urgency. Promise yourself that you'll still address the issue if it needs to be addressed; otherwise, you're just suppressing. In fact, let the person know right now that you want to set a meeting with them in two days. You can strategize later.

Step 3: Stop Blaming and Excusing

The fastest relief ever is to blame someone else. Think back to a recent time when you were done wrong. It feels good to call a friend and have them agree with you about whose fault it is that you flew off in a rage. We all look for social proof that they deserved it because they caused it. *Think of blame as a shortcut for avoiding responsibility.* As long as we blame others, we give others the power over our life circumstances and ultimately our life experience. When we blame others, either consciously or unconsciously, what follows is justification. We make excuses for unproductive behaviors. We say things like "That's just the way I am" and "I'm too old to change now" and "I'm only being honest." When someone says, "That's just the way I am," my question is this: "Is that the way you want to be?" If so, no problem. However, if what you're doing now isn't working, then it's time to make some changes. "But I'm too old to change now, and I've always done it this way." Scientists used to believe that we didn't have the ability to make changes in our brains past a certain age, but now they have uncovered an exciting truth: our brains have plasticity and can change with some practice; we aren't victims to our past ways of being if we want to choose a different path.

QUESTIONS TO ANSWER

1. Who did you blame the last time you got upset?

2. In what way did you also contribute to the situation?

3. What did you do to resolve the issue with this person?

4. In hindsight, how could you have handled the situation better?

If you think someone is at least partially to blame, initiate a conversation with that person to resolve the conflict. If you approach them, what do you want from them? Do you just want to vent? If so, just save it. If you need an apology, say so. If you want them to fix it, be clear about what you need them to do for you. Perhaps you need to learn how to ask for what you want, clarify expectations, or set a boundary. We'll talk more about those skills in later chapters.

Step 4: Tell Yourself the Truth

Suppressing your feelings doesn't change the reality that you feel what you feel, whether it's disappointment, anger, blame, jealousy, or a desire for revenge. Truth telling means you don't pretend, don't suppress, and don't fake it, but there's a caveat: even though emotional integrity is about telling yourself the truth about what you *feel and experience*, emotional integrity doesn't necessarily mean you believe the narrative in your head about what's going on. In fact, emotional integrity and truth telling requires you to give up the need to be right and to get curious about how your mind processes and interprets information. When you have strong feelings about something, it's easy to believe every thought you think. I'm sure you've probably said things like "He did that on purpose" and "She's just trying to irritate me" or "They think they are so smart." Those are just thoughts and interpretations that are open to debate. Here's a clue: every time you think you know someone's intention, challenge yourself and let the other person know what's going on in your mind. It goes like this, "Jack, when you're telling me about all the changes we need to make, it makes me think you don't respect my decision-making. Is that so?" It takes more courage to share what's going on in your head than to lash out because of a perception you concocted.

Remember Leroy and Jack? Leroy thought his son Jack was trying to one-up him, and that thought made him angry. When Leroy got angry, he didn't know how to let the energy pass through, and he didn't know how to identify his own unproductive patterns or question the narrative going on inside his head. Instead, he used the only coping mechanism he had—lashing out. Leroy's ego got in the way of seeing his son as a helper instead of a competitor. It doesn't take a psychotherapist to know that Leroy had some unresolved issues, *but don't we all?* Believing every thought in his head didn't work for Leroy, and it won't work for you. Here's some questions you can ask when you notice your thoughts that contribute to your emotional experience.

QUESTIONS TO ANSWER

1. Do I have all the facts, or is this just a thought?

2. What else might equally be true?

3. What assumptions and judgments am I making about this person?

4. Is there a conversation I need to have but have been avoiding?

For example, if Leroy had any measure of control over his narrative, he might say to himself, "I don't know for sure if Jack is competing with me. Maybe that's my own insecurity and fear of being irrelevant. Jack respects me and wants to be a co-owner one day. Maybe Jack wants my acknowledgment on all that he's working on. Maybe he has business knowledge that will help the company grow." If you can at least entertain two or three more possibilities than the one you currently believe, you're on your way to increasing your emotional integrity through challenging your narrative, rather than being ruled by your unconscious and unproductive thought patterns. There's always time to check in with the other person regarding your perceptions, rather than jumping to conclusions you made when you were high on your own emotions.

Those four steps sound easy, don't they? Everything is easy when it's on a spreadsheet or in a workshop or, in this case, when you read it in a book. What makes most of our decision-making and leadership so difficult are all those messy emotions.

Striving for Authenticity

When you're on the journey to emotional integrity, every bone in your body will work against you. If you hear the voice in your head saying "I just want to be authentic!" it's a sign that you would rather just be right than make the needed changes. That's probably coming from your unconscious brain, which wants to stay comfortably in old patterns. There's a lot of material out there about the benefits of being authentic, and there seems to be a lot of confusion about what it means to be an authentic leader. The question is this: Do you want to be authentic to the childlike, undeveloped part of you that wants to be right, who screams for attention, and who can't manage their inner world—the part of you that's undisciplined, lacks self-regulation, and can't handle disappointment? Or do you want to be authentic to the part of you that wants to live in higher awareness, who makes intentional decisions based on core values? Do you want to be the victim to circumstances or the master of your experience? Do you want to stay where you are, or do you want to grow? Being authentic to your child or being authentic to your adult is simply a matter of alignment and choice. We all have many authentic parts; *the point is, we have to choose which level of authenticity serves us better.* When you say, "I'm just being honest," or "I just want to be authentic," that's when you know there's a part of you that doesn't want to change—the part that wants to be right and make others responsible for your unproductive behavior. Change is so much easier if you have a basic understanding of how the brain works, so that you can make your brain work for you and not against you.

Stop Overcompensating

But wait . . . what about Jack? If you relate more to Jack, you have some serious decisions to make. What narratives do you entertain that keep you from having a serious conversation? What's keeping you from setting stronger boundaries? What ideas are keeping you locked into unequal relationships where you're being disrespected?

If you relate to Jack, realize that you aren't serving yourself or the organization to continue to be a doormat and take abuse. It takes courage to change the narrative that's keeping you imprisoned in unproductive relationships at work or at home.

If others take advantage of you, look at where you're avoiding a conversation with them to set appropriate boundaries. When you see someone who doesn't have emotional integrity, ask yourself if you've been in some small way enabling the very behavior you don't want. Have you been taking on everyone else's emotional work? It takes two to play games unless you're playing solitaire. If you betray yourself to calm the waters, you're still part of the problem—allowing someone to get by with disrespectful or inappropriate behavior just so you can have a moment's peace.

When it comes to conflict, many of us overcompensate when dealing with high-conflict, high-maintenance people or with those who we believe to be overly sensitive. Many of us grew up in households where others tried to make us responsible for situations we couldn't be responsible for. We were told, "You really made your father unhappy," and "I'm disappointed because of a decision you made," and "You're the oldest so you should know better." It's no wonder we take those ideas and try to use them in our leadership roles; it was programmed in. Thank goodness we have choices to rewind and change the old tapes.

What you can do is become a mirror of emotional integrity for your peers, colleagues, and employees. You can set appropriate boundaries and make appropriate choices. What does it take? I'll let the genie out of the bottle: you have to accept them the way they are and stop dreading their inappropriate behavior. In other words, expect the worst. They've already shown you who they are, so why resist it, and why wish it would be better? They are who they are, and right now they see no reason to change. People change because it works for them to change. Your real goal is to act in integrity with your own value system, not to override them, shame them, or make them come to reason. They won't. Remember that.

Trying to change others compromises your emotional integrity. If you're the boss of a high-conflict individual, you can council them and hold them accountable. If they change, it'll be for two reasons: you had the courage to confront the behavioral issues, and they desired personal change. We will talk more about how to do this in chapter 6, on resistance, and chapter 7, on the skill blueprint. If you're a leader with real authority and they refuse to change, you can let them go. You don't have to be held hostage.

If there's an "unregulated" person in your life, whether it be a family member, a boss, a colleague, a board member, or an employee, you'll waste time trying to change them. All you can do is manage the situation by using high emotional integrity. There are multifaceted dynamics within every conflict. For example, Jack was trained in business and had an education in technology and finance. His father was more of a blue-collar bootstrapper used to working with his hands. Jack was more strategic, and Leroy was more tactical. Jack was more brain, and Leroy more brawn. Regarding personality, Jack was more agreeable, Leroy less so. Jack was more open, Leroy was more closed. Jack had an insatiable desire for learning, while his father believed that because he had started the business, he knew more than Jack. Add these differences to the dynamics of a family-owned business, with the father and son relationship, and there are many invisible influences besides communication styles or personality. We can spend lifetimes studying personality theory desiring to understand ourselves and others better. We can take the DiSC assessment, the Myers-Briggs, and the Enneagram to search for answers. No doubt there is value in increased understanding.

Then there's the path of simplicity and clarity. You can make a new decision. You can decide to get clear about who you want to be in the world and then strive to become that every single day, even when you're around high-conflict, high-maintenance, oversensitive people and, yes, even the few who seem clueless.

WHEN IT COMES TO BUILDING EMOTIONAL INTEGRITY, THERE ARE THREE RULES TO LIVE BY:

1. I am responsible for my thoughts, feelings, and actions.

2. Others are responsible for their thoughts, feelings, and actions.

3. Disagreement doesn't ruin relationships, disrespect does.

If you're responsible for your thoughts, feelings, and actions, then it stands to reason that other people are responsible for their thoughts, feelings, and actions. The big mistake is to take on everyone else's feelings. It's OK to be sensitive and strategic, but what I've witnessed when working with leaders is the belief that they have to avoid giving feedback because they feel responsible for someone else's defensiveness or hurt feelings. Allow space for others to feel what they feel without overcompensation, manipulation, or aggression. You don't have to fix them. What they feel is OK, and what you feel is OK. Your feelings belong to you, and their feelings belong to them. This perspective frees all of us. We can still have empathy, curiosity, and understanding, and the more you understand this concept, the more empathetic and understanding you will be because there's nothing to prove anymore. You aren't in a competition to prove a point, get social proof, or be right.

Believing you're 100 percent responsible for your thoughts, feelings, and actions keeps you focused, helps you avoid distractions, and elevates your productivity. You won't have to waste hours on the phone gossiping about what someone did to you. Instead, you'll deal with your narrative, your interpretations, and your feelings, and then you'll take appropriate action with the one person who can work through this issue with you, instead of others who just love to hear you gripe. Instead of holding grudges, you can set boundaries so that you don't allow the inappropriate behavior again. And when you feel taken advantage of, you don't have to play games and offer tit for tat. You can go straight to the person and ask for what you want instead of dredging up the past that you haven't gotten over. If your workplace culture doesn't support these decisions, perhaps you have more important decisions to consider about the type of environment that will help you to thrive.

If disagreement doesn't ruin relationships, then it's OK to disagree. Show respect, especially when you disagree, and even if someone else acts out, don't get distracted because, in the end, everything is circular. You reap what you sow. Emotional integrity is a requirement for building conflict capacity and is a skill that will serve you in every single area of life.

——————————— **Reflection** ———————————

1. Who do you identify with more, Jack or Leroy?

2. What do you need to do to self-regulate?

3. What can you do when working with someone who is not self-regulated?

4. Name a time a disagreement almost ruined a relationship.

   a. What could you have done differently?

   b. How will you handle similar disagreements in the future?

5

Environmental Impact:
Structure Determines Behavior

*Our perceptions and interpretations
create structures of knowing.*

John Andrew Perello, also known as JonOne, was chosen as
one of the graffiti artists to paint a mural to be displayed at
an exhibition in Seoul, South Korea.[1] JonOne, raised in New
York City, grew up believing his work was never really appreciated,
and he experienced that feeling again when his painting was vandalized by a young couple who added a few of their own strokes in
the middle of the painting on display at the World Mall.

Why in the world would a couple deface a piece of artwork
in broad daylight at an international exhibition? Did they think
they could get away with it? Security cameras captured the event,
and the couple were arrested for damaging a painting valued at
$400,000. The painting could eventually be restored but at a cost
of $9,000 and many hours of the artist's time. Should the couple
be held liable, and spend time in jail, or do community service?
Should the insurance company sue the couple to recover part of

the damage? Think about this scenario, and before reading on, give your best answer on what should happen.

Now that you think you know what should happen, let's look at the situation from a different perspective. Suppose the couple didn't intend harm. Suppose they misunderstood what was going on, and while viewing the painting, they noticed the paint cans, the brushes, and a pair of shoes sitting in front of the mural, and they interpreted the paint cans and brushes as an opportunity to participate. So, they grabbed a brush and painted three small strokes covering thirty-five inches by eleven inches of space, adding to the abstract expressionist graffiti. They didn't fully understand the artist's intention to include the shoes, paint, and brushes that he used while working on the project to be part of the artwork itself, not an invitation to participate. From this perspective, the couple were joining in on a public community project.

We don't really know the intention of the couple, maybe they vandalized the painting on purpose, or maybe they made an honest mistake and misread the intention of the artist. The result was the same either way; the artist's work was defaced. Here's the point: our intentions matter. Our perceptions about *other people's intentions* also matter, and when intentions are misrepresented or misunderstood, we potentially create unwanted results. How many of our conflicts are due to someone misunderstanding our intentions? How many conflicts remain unresolved because we've made assumptions about someone else's intentions?

This chapter is about structures and how structure determines behavior. Part of my understanding of structure was influenced by Robert Fritz, author of *The Path of Least Resistance* and *The Path of Least Resistance for Managers*. The definition of "structure" in *The Path of Least Resistance for Managers* is "an entity such as an organization made up of individual elements or parts (such as people, resources, aspirations, values, market trends, levels of competence, reward systems, departmental mandates, capital, workload/capacity, relationships, and so on) that impact each other by the relationships they form." I'd like to simplify the definition of structure as the visible elements and the invisible elements working together to shape culture and drive behavior.

An easy example is to think of a two-story building with a stairway to the second floor. The way you get to the second floor is by taking the stairs. The stairs are a physical structure; the desire to get to the second floor is an invisible structure. If an elevator is installed, there's another structure offering a different choice. If at some point someone got stuck in the elevator, and it had a reputation of being undependable, most people might opt for the stairway. The history and the structures of knowing create another invisible structure that determines behavior. If, as a leader, you understand the visible and invisible structures that shape behavior, you can work with structures to get the results you want.

Visible and Invisible Structures

In JonOne's story, the painting, the location, the shoes, and the open cans of paint were the physical and visible structures. Neither the artist nor the mall wanted the painting to be ruined, but perhaps the structures are partly to blame. Consider the location (a mall instead of a museum), the type of art form (graffiti versus fine art or sculpture), and the open cans of paint, which are the visible structures that somehow influenced invisible structures—the couple's understanding, previous experiences, and interpretation. Perhaps the visible and invisible structures contributed to the couple adding paint to a piece of work that was not their own. *Sometimes it's helpful to consider conflict as opposition due to the visible and invisible structures in play.*

Our perceptions and interpretations create "structures of knowing." The problem with structures of knowing is that my structure of knowing is probably not the same as yours. Our structures of knowing can be drastically different than that of our employees, our clients, our vendors, and our international contacts, unless we have had similar life experiences, opportunities, education, and influences. The human brain automatically creates meaning out of interpretations, all influenced by previous experience. From JonOne's structure of knowing as an artist, he perceived vandalism. Is it possible the couple had a different structure of knowing? Perhaps the couple saw an opportunity to add value and have some fun, or perhaps they saw an opportunity for some mischief and they wanted to take a risk. We don't know for sure. Uncertainty with lack of clarity almost always invites conflict. That's why we have rules and policies in the workplace, to gain clarity on what's expected and what's in bounds or out of bounds. Policies and rules are created to align our structures of knowing. Agreements and contracts do the same in business.

There actually was a policy in place at the mall, a posted sign about the purpose of the exhibit, that was either ignored or misunderstood. Does that remind you of company policies that are shoved into dusty three-ring binders that are no longer noticed and the temptations of the day are too colorful? Sometimes invisible structures, such as beliefs, identity, thoughts, and desires, compete with other invisible structures, such as policies and rules.

Temptation: An Invisible Structure

This brings to mind a memory of doing sanitation at a food plant where I worked night shifts many years ago. We worked from midnight to morning tearing down equipment and then washing it with high-pressure water hoses. We had to bring a change of clothing because we ended up soaking wet from all the water and steam. We weren't supposed to engage in horseplay, and there were plenty of safety policies, safety meetings, and safety practices, but when you've been working doing sanitation for six hours in a hot, steamy room with high-pressure water hoses, it's just too tempting to avoid getting into secret water fights with your coworkers who are craving a little mischief. In the workplace, whether we like it or not, there are invisible structures in play, temptation being one of them, and our thoughts being another.

The point here is that leaders can work with the invisible structures by becoming more aware of and deliberate about how they think, how thoughts manifest into the spoken and written word, and then how the words we hear and see are interpreted by others.

Notice the words I used when writing about the couple and the painting. I used the words *vandalized, ruined,* and *defaced.* Did those words influence you? They might have, if I had not said that we don't know for sure what their intention was—was their action out of spite, the need for mischief, or a misunderstanding?

Leaders can use language, the written and spoken word, as an invisible structure to effectively resolve or manage conflict and motivate employees. A simple example is framing your conversation to be forward moving and positive versus backward moving and negative. Rather than talking about what happened in the past, you talk about the future desired behavior, and instead of saying what you don't want, you speak about what you do want. These simple techniques can be the difference between compliance and commitment from your team. We will explore more of those techniques in chapter 7, when I give you a blueprint for conversations. For now, let's look at some examples of how the physical environment shapes behavior in the workplace.

—————— Case Study: LinkedIn Learning ——————

Imagine a work environment where people step in to help each other out, where there's a combination of high structure with high autonomy and talent is easy to recruit because everyone wants to work there. I've seen that culture, and I've observed the balance of a high work ethic with the agreement that humans need rejuvenation and fun. That organization is LinkedIn Learning in Santa Barbara. LinkedIn Learning is a global organization reaching diverse organizations and people all over the world through their online video education platform with subjects ranging from leadership to construction, sales to project management, and an endless list of titles and subjects, designed by experts and produced in-house.

I've been fortunate enough to design and film several learning videos related to the content of this book, including Difficult Conversations, Anger Management, and Working with High Conflict People, to name a few. As a collaborator and contract worker, I got to see the many parts and pieces and work with all kinds of employees, from producers to videographers to set designers to content managers and beyond. While on location filming my video scripts, I saw observable behaviors—evidence of how the work culture was intentionally designed to keep people motivated, engaged, and happy.

Meals are catered in for all employees and experts who are on location for filming. The food is fresh, organic, and diverse. If you're a vegan, there are vegetables and tofu. If you're a carnivore, there are varieties of chicken, fish, or beef. If you like desserts, try a donut, some cookies, or a cheesecake. Every day there's variety, including soups, breads, and fresh-fruit-infused water. As you finish lunch, you pass by a ping-pong table where a couple of employees are taking a break playing a game.

When you're filming, you might get a text that it's snack-attack time. Snack attacks are when you get surprised with a catered-in snack or sweet treat and all employees stop what they're doing to gather in the cafeteria. If you don't make it to snack attack, you can go into one of the hallways to find fully stocked drawers of snacks like popcorn, organic nuts, protein bars, or gummy bears. You can even take some home. No one is "checking" to make sure you don't steal something or take too much. Needless to say, because the culture is that of an abundance mentality, there's always enough. Brainpower is freed up because you never have to think about what you're going to eat. It's provided. Employees don't mind staying late occasionally because it's OK to take a break or play a game, and besides that, you got finished two hours early yesterday and made it to the beach for the afternoon. The structures in the environment have been intentionally created for employees to be fully supported and love their work. Needless to say, they help each other out in a pinch. They are also extremely generous with outsiders—their contract workers. I've seen hours dedicated to getting a set right—for example, when I said I didn't want to be seated during my video session. In a sense, I really didn't have any choice. They could have overridden my desire and I would have complied with their decision, but they were willing to make a shift to get to an end result that would be best overall. As guilty as I felt, they kept reassuring me. Their culture is set up to be flexible and keep the "talent" happy if it's something within reason and doesn't negatively affect the project or their policies.

———— Intentionally Designing Structure ————

Here's what I learned from that experience. In the workplace, we are all physical beings working in a physical environment, and our physical, visible environments affect our well-being and thus our performance and our ability to get along with each other. I'm not suggesting that ping-pong tables in the breakroom and free food would work for every environment or that the more goodies and perks offered, the less conflict you'll have. What I am saying is that leaders can intentionally design the visible physical structures to make the desired behavior easy and thus shape the types of conflicts that arise.

During the pandemic, I observed the world and all the conflicts arising due to both the visible and invisible structures: the need to work in a different physical environment and the conflict across the world due to mistrust, misinformation, political identities, and outside stressors of uncertainty. Millions across the globe were forced to work from an ill-equipped home environment while juggling opposing drives, desires, and demands of children, homework, and basic financial needs. The point here is that if we can create a sense of stability in the visible physical environment, we can more easily self-manage our inner environment of fear that contributes to dysfunction and mismanagement.

As an author and consultant, I've always worked from a home office and been mobile enough to work while traveling. I've used virtual systems for well over a decade and worked globally because of the power of technology. When my business friends wondered why I didn't feel as much stress as so many who worked at brick-and-mortar businesses, I knew it wasn't because I was so special or had learned how to self-regulate to that extent. It was because my environment was still intact. Even though I faced the real possibility of losing my business, my environment was stable, and this stability allowed me the space to reset and redesign some of my offerings and expect the best even when everything around me was in a state of uncertainty. My home office has all the capabilities to help me be productive. I have a separate space for work with doors and even a room to do larger projects. I have all the equipment I need to operate without missing a beat.

A complaint from midlevel managers and employees alike is "It feels like we are drifting out to sea in a rudderless ship." What this means is there is a lack of stability due to a lack of certainty. There is value in leaders creating a sense of stability inside the physical environment and, in the *invisible realm*, by the language we use and the behaviors we exhibit. Stop for a moment and ask this question: What resources do we need right now that would help stabilize the environment and make it more conducive to getting our end result without unnecessary conflict? It could be a catered meal on deadline days. It could mean offering flextime as long as the work gets done. It could mean offering some sort of perk like a shuttle to get people to work from a large parking lot, or an on-site childcare service for shift workers. The ideas are endless. It's not about the cost; it's about the value and the return on investment. Look at the tardiness, the conflicts, or the poor productivity as a sign that something isn't working in the immediate environment, and ask yourself if there's any opportunity to work with existing structures to make the environment better or reduce conflict. Could we find the budget for additional resources that add more value in the long run? What behaviors are we trying to encourage or discourage, and how does structure contribute? Are there innovative ways to support the physical needs of your workers and future leaders?

It's empowering to know that leaders can work with the structures to make the workplace more comfortable for employees so they appreciate their jobs and are more likely to engage. I've worked in departments doing sanitation where the temperature was over a hundred degrees and we had to wear uniforms and hairnets. There was no relief and, from our perspective as frontline workers, no compassion for our discomfort. From where we worked, we could see in the glass-encased office the managers working in the comfort of air-conditioning. Even a rotation where we got a break to go into the air-conditioned office would have been a thoughtful way to compensate for the reality of the job we had to do. There were times when power struggles broke out all because there weren't enough chairs to do the rote work comfortably. Some employees would sneak in early to steal the chairs of another line. These conflicts weren't about personality. We didn't need a workshop on building character or personality assessments to "figure each other out" or a motivational speech to figure out *why* we do the work we do. We didn't need online lessons in how to stop workplace drama. Our issues could have been solved by working with the structures—for example, changing rotations, buying a few extra chairs, providing breaks for relief.

With just a tad bit of insight and leadership, these conflicts could have been resolved. The point I'm making here isn't to compare professional work with blue-collar work, or to complain about a past life that I chose. The point is that there are always ways to make the environment better, no matter the type of organization. It just takes some courage and some leadership.

—————— Decision-Making as a Structure ——————

By making strategic decisions, leaders ultimately shape behaviors—not only inside their organization but how their customers, patients, and clients behave. Let's take a look at a common example as we explore the concept that structure determines behavior. At Aldi grocery store, you never see a cart in the middle of the parking lot, but at other stores, carts are strewn all across the lot on a busy shopping day. What's the difference? The difference is structure. Aldi (the leadership team) has consciously shaped structure to save money and determine shoppers' behavior through their decision-making about carts. Aldi shapes consumer behavior by charging a fee to use the cart. It's only twenty-five cents, but when you return the cart, you get your quarter back. There's a payoff for doing what the store wants you to do: return the cart. No more customers complaining about the parking lot. No more difficult conversations with employees who don't take initiative to retrieve carts. As an organization, Aldi saves money by not having to hire employees to clean the parking lots.

In contrast, look at Walmart. On a hectic day, carts are strewn all over the parking lot, and even though employees gather the carts, sometimes they get busy and the parking lot is a mess. Some customers do return carts, even if they park far away and it's raining. Why? The invisible structures at play: identity, beliefs, and values. Those who return carts see themselves as responsible citizens, role models for their children, or they value respect, and by putting a cart back, they're in alignment with their values.

Recently I got a call from a senior leader wondering what to do about clients who were taking advantage of their project managers, going behind their backs with unreasonable demands, working the system for their own gains, breaking the agreements set in place. As you can imagine when conflicts erupt between employees and unreasonable clients, decision-making becomes tricky unless you align with the agreements put in place and the values of the organization. In these types of situations, the opposing drives, desires, and demands are clearly in competition. On the one hand, you want to keep clients happy, but on the other hand, you don't want employees to perceive they're being mistreated. When the client demands outweigh the available resources to meet demands, it's time for difficult conversations, course corrections, and boundary setting.

In this case, my client was seeking a workshop for project managers on how to set boundaries with their clients. The real issue here was that the leadership team needed to revisit and clarify agreements with clients so they could keep delivering superior service. The senior leaders told me they were ready to back their employees, but I challenged them. Would they really? What if a client threatened to leave? What if the employee boundary was viewed as "rebelliousness" or a lack of customer service? This is how standing firm on values and promises shapes culture. If employees go out on a limb and set boundaries, only to be dismissed after the client pulls the power cord, what kind of culture is being created for the future?

As you know by now, the first step is always leadership clarity: identity the current position, the desired outcome, and the obstacles to getting there. In this case, the client's expectation is the obstacle, and the leaders need to take a stand to initiate conversations to create a path for employees. Then and only then can the employees securely set boundaries and keep them. Going out of order when power struggles erupt between high-stakes clients and midlevel employees is a recipe for disaster. Leaders shape employee behavior and build structures to get the desired client behaviors. People do what works for them depending upon the structures they are in. What works for any one of us in any given situation is what's easiest, what we get by with, what values motivate us, or what aligns with the outcomes we want.

Leaders and leadership teams in every type of industry influence the structure that shapes culture, for the good and for the bad, either intentionally or by default. Just look at any executive team, board of directors, city council, or government, and there's plenty of examples of great success stories or miserable failures.

It's a good practice, when talking about leadership, to distinguish between a single leader in a department, a team of leaders, or a governing body of leaders, such as a board of directors. Individual leaders influence their teams, as well as their individual area of authority. Before talking about character traits, personality, or charisma, it's important to talk about how leadership is defined and selected when it comes to choosing an individual leader for a particular role or position. Many organizations I've worked with didn't create a working definition for leadership, and as a result, the selection of leaders is often the wrong fit. Frontline supervisors are chosen based on a particular skill set or on seniority. As a result, many of the skills new leaders need to effectively manage conflict and navigate through difficult situations are missing, putting the company at future risk. At the highest levels of leadership, including C-suite, board members, and business partners, leaders are selected for their business savvy, financial acumen, or deep connections, often without considering cultural alignment. It's a mistake to look only at opportunity when choosing powerful partners or positions, without considering cultural fit. When politics and personalities come into play, opportunity without alignment causes internal power struggles that are difficult to resolve.

Invisible Structures: Definitions, Power, Behavior

Crafting a strong definition for what it means to be a leader in your organization and aligning that definition with a set of core values *creates a strong invisible structure* from the beginning. If the leader is defined only by role or by one narrow outcome—for example, sales, higher profits, more market share—in the future there will be dramatic conflicts that cannot be resolved easily. At the highest level of leadership, these conflicts cause the most confusion due to a disconnect between leadership behavior and core values.

Recently, Robert, a colleague of mine, and I were talking about the behavior of a senior-level leader, Thomas, who had been hired by the CEO of a fast-growing small enterprise. Thomas had a lot of business savvy, deep connections, and external power—he was a well of knowledge about the industry and a valuable resource to the organization. The problem was that Thomas offended many of the new senior women leaders. He was brash, told it like it is, and didn't care about hurting feelings. He brushed off any complaint as "them having thin skin" rather than thinking he needed to make some shifts. He seemed to be proud of his radical candor, often used without any sensitivity to how other people perceived him or how harsh his criticism came off. One of the senior women leaders complained about the behavior and felt that she had an ally in Robert, but in truth, she knew that Robert couldn't fight her battles. Robert, feeling like he was in the middle, didn't know strategically how to handle the problem, and that's when he reached out for some advice. He thought it might be helpful to offer coaching to the senior woman leader to help her toughen up or to know what to say in response to Thomas's brash remarks, but this is a values issue, not a communication skills issue.

Where power structures are concerned, nothing is going to change as long as excuses about rude behavior is the norm. Ignoring or offering just the right remark or comeback goes only so far when there's an imbalance of power within the structure of leadership. Unbridled power never wants to course correct itself. What balances this type of structure is the invisible structure of a shared set of values and a system of accountability to ensure commitment.

Obviously, it's better if the values are decided in advance rather than looked at after the fact. In one particular case, an organization had a set of values, at least seven, two of which were integrity and candor. At times these two values seemed to be in opposition. For example, one executive had no trouble with candor, but he didn't temper his candor with kindness, and some of his behaviors seemed to be out of integrity to other values. Instead, he made excuses and justified rude behavior.

Unless the elephant of misaligned values is addressed, excuses will continue. You can do a workshop, you can offer coaching, and you can facilitate a retreat with your people, but these initiatives clear the air for only a day. You can't solve this type of problem without looking at leadership and decision-making as part of the invisible structures of accountability or lack thereof.

Leaders have the most influence on shaping the culture either consciously or unconsciously. Leaders make decisions. Leaders have final say. Leaders have access to resources, power, budget. The decisions a leader makes and the way a leader behaves betray their strengths, weaknesses, and ultimately, their values. Leaders who show up late, lose their temper, allow poor performance, act arrogantly, ignore problems, and the like will almost always blame employees and wonder why things are the way they are. They often aren't able to retain the best employees because the best employees get tired of ineffective leadership and they find employment elsewhere.

A tell-tale sign of a leader who lacks self-awareness is their belief that *business growth equals personal growth*. I make a distinction between the two. Business growth is about the numbers: the hard skills, market share, revenue growth, and all qualities that define traditional success. When success as a leader is measured only in terms of shareholder value, sales, top-line growth—in other words, the outer game of success—there's often no emphasis on principles such as character, integrity, and trust, or no attention paid to people skills. Those focused exclusively on business growth view the hustle of opportunity as a higher value than the discipline of alignment. They often don't see that the many unhealthy conflicts are not because of bad employees but because of the ineffective leadership and misaligned decision-making. Working for this kind of leader is like rowing a boat with dozens of holes in its bottom. They push relentlessly no matter what the cost.

On the other side of the spectrum is the leader who is both business-growth minded and personal-growth minded. The personal-growth leader takes time to reflect and is interested in understanding the invisible structures of values, principles, and vision. They are skilled communicators, they show empathy, and they're interested in growing others. They hold values like trust, integrity, and collaboration as top priorities. They have a strong leadership identity as opposed to a strong identity tied to egoic needs. They understand that behavior is part of performance, not separate from it. They work on their inner game as much as they work on their outer game. They model the behaviors they want from their employees instead of making excuses as to why they are the exception. They realize that their decisions and actions have the power to shape culture.

Shadow of the Leader

There's a concept called the "shadow of the leader," which means that the leader casts a shadow on the organization. There's no choice in the matter about whether a shadow will be cast, but there is a choice on what kind of shadow is cast: a shadow of dysfunction and drama, or a shadow of productivity, innovation, and collaboration. This concept applies even to more complex systems—for example, an executive director of a nonprofit is a leader, but this leader also reports to the "will of the board," which is a group of leaders. The relationship dynamics between leaders and groups of leaders cast a pretty big shadow, so it's prudent to understand how a leader's or a team of leaders' behaviors shape the culture. Leadership groups as well as individual leaders shape culture either consciously or unconsciously. When this concept is understood, leaders can consciously shape the culture into the desired mindsets and behaviors, rather than leaving culture influence to chance. If you happen to be a leader on a team of other leaders, you can at least start observing the behaviors of the team at large to address the issues that need to shift in order to get the desired outcomes.

Actions speak louder than words. When the actions of the top leaders do not align with the company values, people notice. When respect is a top value but the senior leaders talk down to their associates or use sarcasm or name call, this sends a message to the employees that this leader is not to be trusted.

—————— Leadership Behavior and Culture ——————

I worked with an organization that was dealing with some serious complaints about Mitch, who was great at managing up. He got things done, and he treated his superiors like the most important people on earth. His vice president, Daniel, never doubted Mitch's abilities, until a second complaint crossed his desk that warranted further investigation of Mitch's leadership. The way Mitch treated his superiors was different from the way he treated employees. This was quite a shock to Daniel, who had been more of a hands-off leader because he trusted his director. With some research and investigation, it became clear that Mitch had a command-and-control style of leadership. While he was good at change management in the early years, once things calmed down, those same skills he used for reorganization weren't conducive to a harmonious work environment. Mitch often threatened employees with losing their jobs even though they had been employed for decades. He told them, "No one will ever believe you because I'm in good with the higher-ups." In the interviews, I learned that Mitch used harsh joking, name-calling, shaming, and retaliation to keep everyone in line. And if you think it's just "women who have drama," think again. The people I interviewed were all men! The point I'm making is that these are *people issues*, and if you know how to look and listen, unresolved conflict is everywhere in every industry with every gender.

The stereotypes we buy into make it all the more difficult to be discerning. Aggressive men often get a pass for being assertive while women are judged harshly for having strong opinions. If a woman cries, it's considered normal, but if a man cries, he can be perceived as too sensitive. The fact is, we're all human and we all have a range of emotions available to us; we simply express differently depending upon our wiring and history. We all have biases that are unexamined and unfair. The good news is that we are becoming more aware of our underlying assumptions, stereotypes, and biases. We all have a lot of work to do to challenge and break down our outdated structures of knowing and perceiving.

Although actions speak louder than words, words give away secrets if you know how to listen. Listen for any hint of blame instead of shared responsibility. Another red flag is justifying. Recently I heard a C-level leader justify his habit of showing up late and in the same breath make an excuse for not paying attention at a retreat. His language indicated that he saw himself as more important and much too busy to be present, while the employees saw him as undisciplined and incongruent. If we buy into the blame or excuses, we aren't seeing the behavior. I noticed how this leader's executive team seemed to buy into the excuses—after all, it's their job to support their leader—but the challenge before them was to bring the elephant into the room. We communicate whether we want to or not. As leaders, we have to be conscious that the intended message is the message received. The higher the leadership, the more power you have, but every leader has some power within their own area of influence.

Reflection

1. How do the invisible structures of behavior, power, or language affect your workplace?

2. How do your structures of knowing serve you?

3. When have your structures of knowing contributed to conflict?

4. How do the physical structures in your workplace affect the following?

    a. Employees

    b. Leaders

    c. Clients

6

Resistance Training: Working with High-Conflict People

*Disruptive people will continue
to be disruptive as long as no one
has the courage to confront them.*

Sherri B., a female consultant working in the male-dominated industry of public safety, found it easy to go head to head with powerful, aggressive commissioners like Mr. Mason. Mr. Mason was known for being a contrarian at the board of county commissioner meetings, sharing his opinions as if they were facts and using intimidation and strong posturing to sway votes to make sure taxes were never raised—ever. By the time Sherri was hired to assess deficiencies, no improvements had been made in decades even at the request of those working directly in the 911 center. As a result, the center was understaffed and the networks and technology outdated. There was a need for more employees, but the dispatchers had outgrown their dark basement, and there just wasn't any room. The county commissioners were detached and uninformed, until Sherri delivered the bad news: "Here I was telling the board that they needed four things: more staffing, a new building, new networks, and infrastructure support, which would require a big budget, and increasing budgets always means raising taxes."

As Sherri presented, she noticed that most of the commissioners seemed caught off guard, some of them shaking their heads in surprise and a few nodding in agreement, except for Mr. Mason, who sat there with a sour look on his face, eyes closed, and arms crossed. Sherri proceeded to deliver the estimated costs based on recommendations, and after a brief pause, Mr. Mason threw his pen on the table, reared back in his chair, pointed his finger at Sherri, and asked, "Well, where do you think we're going to get this big pot of gold?"

Without missing a beat, Sherri B. said, "Mr. Mason, that's your decision. My job was to do the investigation and deliver the information to you." Boom!

Sherri didn't take the bait. She didn't get defensive. She didn't get her feelings hurt. She stayed grounded and focused, even though she felt frustrated. Sherri wasn't intimidated by a councilman who didn't want to hear about raising taxes. How did she do it? Sherri told me, "As a consultant I've been trained to stay within the scope of project and stay dispassionate. I'm there to focus and get the job done."

Most of us get nervous when we face off with aggressive people, when we get caught off guard or feel misunderstood. Emotions magnify when we are working with high-profile people that we consider to be difficult or demanding. Before we go any further, let's revisit a rule of human nature: disruptive people will continue to be disruptive as long as no one has the courage to confront them. The workplace bully, the unconscious, the contentious, behave as they do because they've gotten away with it so far. With some courage, skills, and accountability, a leader with enough conflict capacity can turn this ship around if the difficult person happens to be an employee. However, when the less-than-agreeable person has power and authority, there's no catalyst for change. Very few of us are born with the wisdom, courage, or resistance training necessary to right the ship. In Sherri's case, she's not Mr. Mason's colleague or employee. Sherri is an outsider—a consultant hired to do a job—but when you must deliver unwanted news, it still takes a tough skin and a great deal of conflict capacity to work around aggressive or immovable individuals who hold a lot of power. No matter what the power structure, coming up against heavy resistance takes a mental and emotional toll.

Disruptive behaviors contribute to a lot of team drama and dysfunction, including poor decision-making. If you've been in the workplace long enough, you've witnessed unproductive conflict in politics, city councils, local governments, and boards of directors. There's often at least one or two aggressive or disagreeable individuals like Mr. Mason who nonetheless are brilliant, are well connected, and have deep pockets and plenty of yes-people around them. Their power is all-consuming, and even if you think they're a complete jerk, it seems to make more sense to go along than to shout out "The emperor has no clothes!" and risk your reputation or career.

Power structures notwithstanding, over the course of your lifetime, you're going to work with colleagues, employees, and bosses that seem difficult to get along with—individuals you experience to be disagreeable, resistant, or high conflict—and you will resist them. You will resist pushing back. You will resist being honest. You will resist almost anything that causes you to feel the inner conflict of working with people you don't like or don't respect. There's another way to see these hard-to-work-with people. These people are precisely the people who showed up in your life to give you what you need most: the courage to expand your conflict capacity. In order to expand capacity for working with difficult people, you need resistance training. That's what this chapter is all about.

Identifying Resistance

Resistance is the nonacceptance of what is and the inability or the unwillingness to make a powerful choice. We humans spend a lot of our time in resistance by not accepting things as they are. As a result, we see ourselves as a victim, instead of seeing ourselves as powerful creators who have many choices. For example, we constantly complain about the weather. In the winter it's too cold, and in the summer it's too hot. It's too windy, it's raining, and it's too cloudy. We complain even when the weather is normal for the season. The point here is that when we can't make peace with reality and we continue to want something or someone else to change and we don't see our own choices, we're in a state of resistance. This doesn't mean that we accept situations that are worth fighting for. Taking a positive action toward a better future for yourself or for others is not resistance. Complaining about the situation and giving up is.

Giving up and pretending you don't care is just another form of resistance. If you don't like something and there is something you can do, you must do it, but you must not complain about things over which you have absolutely no control. You can't make the sun stop beating down, and you can't require the rain to stop. If you're too hot, get in the shade or go home. If it's raining, you can find shelter or grab an umbrella. You don't always have to understand someone else's decisions. You don't need to get others to agree with you all the time. You don't have to be rude to someone else just because they were rude to you. You have choices in almost every situation. Wisdom is the difference between knowing what we must accept and what we can do to change that which we can't. Resistance slows us down mentally, emotionally, and spiritually. If there's no other lesson to learn in this chapter, it's how to identify and release resistance.

Resistance shows up in a multitude of ways, some easy to identify and some more subtle. Here's a short list:

→ Complaining

→ Negativity

→ Blaming

→ Resentment

➡ Game playing

➡ Noncompliance

➡ Disrespect

➡ Excuses

➡ Innuendos

These thinking and feeling patterns easily leak out behaviorally as incivility, avoidance, and aggression. In conflictual relationships, you'll uncover pockets of resistance, yet resistance doesn't even have to involve other people. You can be in a state of resistance without anyone else even being involved. These thoughts, feelings, attitudes, and behaviors affect our well-being, our productivity, and our results.

SAND

An easy way to identify resistance is to look for four patterns: stuck, attached, negative, and distracted (SAND). Think of being slowed down because you're stuck in the sand. While the SAND patterns are not completely distinct from each other, it's helpful to look a little closer at how resistance shows up as a state of being stuck, attached, negative, and distracted.

Stuck

Being stuck is always a sign of resistance. Should I, or shouldn't I? If I do this, then that will happen, but if I do that, then this will happen. The experience of being stuck is distinct from procrastination. When we're stuck, we waste a lot of time trying to figure something out with no resolution, and brainpower is spent trying to come to resolution. With procrastination, you know you're putting something off, but the thing you're putting off isn't necessarily taking up all of your brainpower. You aren't stewing about it because you have a deadline, and you know you'll eventually get around to it. Stuckness occurs when there's less certainty and more risk. *Being stuck is about putting off making a decision, while procrastination is about waiting to act on a decision that has already been made.*

I've seen consultants waste hours earnestly trying to help a client make a clear choice, only to end up frustrated because of the severity of the resistance. Sometimes the resistance is due to overwhelm. There's a potential future vision that, while desirable, seems overly complicated, risky, or uncertain. My advice is to stop entertaining the conversation after fifteen minutes. Continuing to go back and forth means there is either more research to do, more facts to gather, or more courage to take. When you find yourself stuck, even one small action, such as gathering research, is better than endlessly hashing out the variables. At some point, a decision has to be made or the decision will be made by default. At the core of being stuck is the fear of making a mistake or the need to be perfect.

Getting Unstuck

Feeling stuck is often related to the fear of other people's judgment. Sometimes we can't hear our own voice because too many people have too many opinions. If you want to get unstuck, do these three things:

1. Be willing to be wrong.

2. Seek additional information.

3. Take one small action.

Let me expand for a moment. One, you must *give up the need to be right* if you want to move forward. As long as the issue isn't life threatening. If you trust yourself, you can almost always course correct, and if you're that scared, stop and focus on something else. You'll never know the outcome of the choice you did not take. Two, *get the facts*, seek out some expertise, weigh the risks, act, and then course correct as needed. The same applies when you're stuck in an argument. When two people go back and forth arguing because they need to be right, an easy way to save time is to be willing to be wrong, especially when the argument is irrelevant or insignificant. I'm not suggesting you appease someone else. Just get curious and say, "I could be wrong; let's check to be sure." I've seen managers argue about whether they filed a report in April or May, when all they needed to do was stop playing verbal ping-pong and look up the record to confirm an easy-to-verify fact. Three, *take one action* to move yourself off the hamster wheel. Through one small action, you will discover other pertinent information.

QUESTIONS TO HELP YOU GET UNSTUCK

1. What decision are you trying to make but keep going back and forth on?

2. What barrier is in the way?

3. What facts do you need to move forward?

4. What one small action will you take to move forward to a decision?

5. What's the deadline for your decision?

PRACTICE

Practice saying, "It's OK to make a mistake. I can always course correct." Instead of continuing to talk about how stuck you are, say, "I'm exploring XYZ . . ."

Attached

Anytime you've heard an employee say, "That's not the way my last supervisor did it," they're attached to the past. When you can't recover from disappointment, that's evidence that you were very attached to the vision you had that didn't materialize.

Disappointment is difficult for all of us, and when we're attached to *how it used to be* or *how it should be*, our resistance slows us down from moving forward. Attachments are like addictions. Most of us have plenty of addictions. We are addicted to winning at all costs, to looking good, and even to negative habits like being angry or arguing all the time. You get an idea in your head of how things are going to be, and when reality doesn't match up, it feels bad. That's attachment, the inability to face disappointment. If you see a certain pattern occurring again and again, it's most likely an attachment to something—a need that is unmet. Attachment often happens because we don't understand the difference between *want* and *need*. Wanting something helps us experience the wonderful feeling of desire and anticipation, but when we feel that we *need* something, the advancement, the yes, the agreement, the contract, we set ourselves up for unnecessary suffering. You can want something and maintain your commitment without basing your entire identity on the outcome. When you need something, you lose perspective, discernment, and peace of mind.

The fastest way to let go of attachments is to accept the situation right as it is. You don't need to deny that the situation makes you unhappy. In fact, accept that you don't feel good. Stop judging yourself for your current state of mind. Accept the current reality and stop living in the past or in the fantasy world of what you wish would happen. The faster you accept a situation, the quicker you can take choices to change what you can. The second thing you can do is distinguish want from need. You'll still be OK if you don't get all your wants, but when you need something, it tends to threaten your identity.

IDENTIFY YOUR ATTACHMENTS

1. Who do you argue with the most?

2. Is the argument relevant or petty?

3. How do you respond to disappointment?

4. Did you have a plan B?

5. What do you need to accept to move forward?

PRACTICE

Listen to others instead of demanding they listen to you. Practice saying, "I could be wrong . . ." instead of "I know I'm right . . ." Say, "Walk me through your thought process. . ." instead of shutting down.

Negative

Negativity is a sure sign of resistance. Some people are naturally more negative than others, but most of us have a negative bias. The negative comment sticks like glue, and the ten positive comments slide off us like oil, and our negativity spreads like a virus. You'll see that rule in play when you give a sensitive employee some performance feedback that's neutral to you but devastates the employee because of one tiny, fixable issue. The more we complain, the more neuro-connections we create for the purpose of complaining. That's how the brain works. Have you noticed that being around complainers stirs you up and makes you feel bad? That's why it's so important for leaders to manage their outlook and language and then to course correct negative conversations to positive outcomes. Constant complaining is a sign of nonacceptance, where we are *stuck* in a habit of judging reality and attached to our view of how it should be, just like looking at the cranky board member and thinking they shouldn't be so opinionated, so we gossip with other members who agree.

The quickest way to stop the negativity is to stop giving it energy. Again, this doesn't mean you deny the unfortunate reality, whatever it might be, but stop feeding the beast. What you focus on expands. Where you put your attention is where you put your energy. "But I just need to vent," you say. Did you know that venting creates more connections in the brain for venting? It's true that we all need to be heard and acknowledged, and sometimes we need someone to hear our side of a story. My rule is venting is helpful if it's five minutes and harmful if it's five hours. Pick an amount of time you allow yourself to vent and an amount of time you're willing to engage with someone else in their drama. Let them know this in advance, and you'll have a very workable agreement on how to support each other without both of you going down the drain at the same time.

ELIMINATE NEGATIVITY

1. What do you often complain about?

2. What kind of negativity is circling around your workplace?

3. What kind of worries do you experience on a regular basis?

4. How often do you engage in negative conversations?

PRACTICE

→ Pick something you complain about daily, and decide to stop completely for a week.

→ When you hear someone complain, simply say, "I'm sorry" or "I hear you."

→ Instead of talking about what you don't want, switch it to "what I do want."

Distracted

Most of us resort to distraction when we don't like what we're experiencing. We use gambling, drinking, eating, and shopping to put off making difficult decisions, filling out complex paperwork, or initiating difficult conversations. Your employees are no different from you. Think about a time you were talking with an employee and thought you were on track but they threw you a boomerang and said something like, "That's not fair" and "If you only knew what everyone else thought about your leadership." If you don't identify distractions right when they happen, you're going to wind up ninety degrees off course from your destination, participating in a game of verbal ping-pong and distraction that goes like this:

Them: "Yes, I did."

You: "No, you didn't."

Them: "That's not fair!"

You: "I knew you'd say that."

Them: "Everyone else agrees with me."

You: "Who do you mean?"

Them: "Evelyn said you didn't have enough experience . . ."

You are now engaged in a different conversation than the one you planned for and you're heading to the island called That's Not Fair (see figure 5). It's easy to blame the other person's resistance. Let's look back at Sherri's story. Mr. Mason was in a high state of resistance, he was stuck on his old ideas about not raising taxes, and he was attached to being right. When he got angry, he threw out an insincere question to bait Sherri into an argument. Remember that anger is energy that wants to go somewhere. Had Sherri taken the bait, she could have argued, spent time trying to convince Mr. Mason those taxes needed to be raised, or had a million other conversations that could have escalated. *People will use distraction when they are in high states of resistance.* You better know how to recognize the distraction.

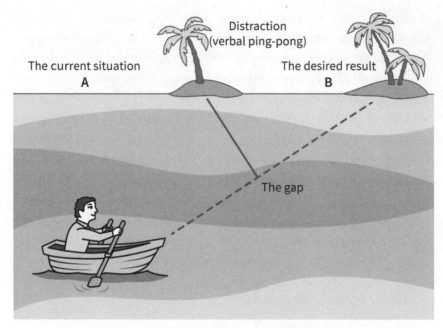

**FIGURE 5. Verbal ping-pong and distraction
(the island called That's Not Fair)**

If you suddenly realize you have gone down a different path than intended in a conversation, just know your counterpart used distraction to avoid hearing what they didn't want to hear and feeling what they didn't want to feel. *But the real problem isn't their efforts to distract you. The real problem is you took the bait. You got distracted.* You just had to engage. You wanted them to understand your point of view. You wanted their agreement, and you got angry when they didn't want to agree or understand. Know this: they probably didn't distract you intentionally. Distraction is an unconscious defense mechanism to put off that which is uncomfortable. But whether they distracted you unconsciously or intentionally, you allowed yourself to entertain their conversation and you didn't know how to redirect.

The best way to avoid distraction is to get agreement about the content of the conversation before you start, and then redirect when it goes off course. This method of getting agreement and redirecting works equally well in meetings with written agendas as it does for difficult conversations when the stakes are high and disagreement is inevitable. It goes like this: "My intention for this conversation is to look at our sales numbers and see where you need support to reach your goals." Then if the conversation goes south, you simply say, "It sounds like that's important, and I'm willing to talk about it later, but our agreement for *this* meeting is . . ." We will talk further about the power of setting intentions in the next chapter, where I'll give you a blueprint for difficult performance or behavioral conversations. The point here is don't start a difficult conversation about sensitive subjects without thinking it through because you will get distracted if you don't strategize first.

IDENTIFY DISTRACTIONS

1. Do you often find yourself derailed in a conversation?

2. How often do you lose focus when in a conversation?

3. When do you engage in verbal ping-pong?

PRACTICE

If you ask a question and your counterpart throws out a distraction, redirect by saying, "That's not the question. The question is . . ." If you find yourself going way off base, course correct by saying, "I'm sorry, I'm getting distracted. What I want to focus on is . . ." If you're in a group setting and the conversation is getting off track, gently nudge the conversation back by saying, "I've noticed we've drifted off course. I'd love to get back on track and talk about XYZ . . ."

Almost any negative energy is related to some form of resistance, the nonacceptance of what is. You now have at your disposal the SAND acronym (stuck, attached, negative, and distracted), and most of the time they are not as clearly defined as I made them here. Anytime you see complaining, blaming, resentment, game playing, harsh judgment, innuendos, and excuses, there's resistance. You are out of the positive flow of productivity. Resistance feels bad.

Three Types of Resistance

There are three forms of resistance: your resistance, their resistance, and your resistance to their resistance. You can work on only your resistance and your resistance to their resistance. Two out of three ain't bad, as the old saying goes. Let's make a few distinctions and then break it down.

Your Resistance

When you're resistant, notice that you're stuck, attached, negative, or distracted. By the act of noticing your own resistance, you can accept things the way they are in reality and free yourself to make a new choice to move forward. Notice when you feel desperate or out of flow, and you'll see that you confused need and want. Make the distinction between need and want and see how much this reduces unnecessary inner conflict.

You no longer need all your employees to agree with your decision-making. Sure, you want them to, but if they don't, it's OK. You don't even need Jamie to come in on time because you've already set the expectation, you're willing to set the consequences for tardiness, and it's OK if Jamie says you're unfair. You have emotional integrity and leadership clarity. You notice where you got a little attached and thought you needed certain things from others to be a good leader. You now realize you just want these things, but you have a job to do and that job isn't about people pleasing. This is your home base—releasing your own resistance—because in the end it's always about your inner landscape and you're the one responsible for your experiences.

Not everyone wants to work on releasing their own resistance. These are the people who have no real reason to change. They aren't concerned about being a more enlightened leader; they are concerned with external authority and power. They seek change from others, and that's why they use intimidation, bullying, victim narratives, and other means to change other people. Releasing resistance requires a certain level of desire and self-awareness, found, in fact, in the very kind of person who is attracted to this kind of book. Don't worry if the Mr. Mason in your life isn't interested in changing. That doesn't belong to you. Look at him as someone in your life who is there to help you grow, gain courage, and transform yourself. Don't judge the Mr. and Ms. Masons in your life. Accept them for where they are now.

The more you resist, the more you take yourself down the hill, and you're going to have to climb that hill at some point, so it's best to always look in the mirror and ask, "What am I resisting?" rather than asking what they are resisting. When you have relationship conflict with a resistant person, it will always seem like it's them, but believe me, it's you. It's always you. Yes, I know they're frustrating. I get it that they're not aware and not motivated, but stop focusing on them and instead focus on yourself. What can you do? What are your choices? When you really learn how to release resistance, you'll free up so much energy and you won't get caught in conflicts you can't win. You won't waste time. You'll set better boundaries. You'll be more direct in asking for what you want, and you'll make cleaner decisions.

Sometimes we mistake a firm no or a strong boundary as "their resistance," but quite the contrary, a strong no is a sign of clarity. If they were indecisive and couldn't give you a straight answer, that's a sign of resistance. As I said, resistance wastes lots of valuable time. Now, *you* might feel resistant to someone else's boundary or their strong no, but they're not the one in resistance, *you are*. They are clear, and you are the one who is attached to a fantasy that they were going to say yes. Misunderstanding resistance and who is the resistant one causes a lot of unnecessary conflict.

High-level sales professionals intuitively understand the dynamics of time-wasting resistance probably more than any other group of professionals on the planet. Experienced sales professionals prefer a clean and clear no than to be given mixed messages as to why the decision is on hold. While a good sales professional might continue to follow up, there wouldn't be a lot of time-wasting attachments about what should happen. They move on and don't get in their own way. They don't take on the resistance of the other person who won't make a decision. They're focused on outcomes, not on making someone do something they don't want to do or can't do. When they conclude that they're wasting time, they keep the relationship going but they don't keep pressuring the stuck person. They don't let someone else's resistance become their resistance. So how do you tell where the resistance is? Is it them, is it you?

Their Resistance

You can't do anything about *their resistance*. You'll meet strong personalities on a board of directors in C-suite roles, and even some of your colleagues will display resistance. They'll be negative, closed minded, argumentative, and stubborn. If you can observe them instead of judging them, you'll conserve a lot of energy. Stop avoiding their responses, just be OK with how they might respond and let them do what they do. Set a boundary if you need to, but otherwise just observe and get curious. It's not that difficult if you aren't attached to them being the way you want them to be. And you might be surprised how some acceptance of them goes a long way in building better relationships with them. You're going to see resistant employees who have so much potential but who won't do the work, and this will cause you some inner conflict, but you shouldn't resist their choices. Your choice is to talk with them, coach them, put them on a suspension, or let them go. But the moment you start caring more than they do, you're entering into the third category of resisting their resistance. It's very difficult to be around resistant people whom you care about and not get entangled in their resistance. In the workplace, and for you as a leader, your best tools here are boundary setting and accountability. You don't need to keep convincing someone who doesn't want to grow or change, to grow or change. They have to want their success more than you want their success. You want them to see the light—but you don't need them to. They have choices, and you also have choices.

Resisting Their Resistance

I used to avoid conversations with my husband about changes I wanted to make to the house because "I already knew what he was going to say." I resisted his resistance. The problem was, we hadn't even had the conversation yet, but I had plenty of grudges because of past experiences that I didn't want to repeat. I wasn't OK with him saying no to things I wanted. I was afraid of the conflict, so I avoided, or I made unilateral decisions and then apologized later. Not a great way to build trust. So, if there's an ask you want to make, go ahead and make it. They might say no. But they might say "Tell me more," or they might say maybe, or they might say yes. Oh, I know, it's easier to be resentful before they ever have a chance to reject you. You'll make up all kinds of reasons why you haven't asked yet, and you get to be right about it. Your willingness to risk rejection is your badge of courage.

Besides, if they actually do reject your request, you can blame me for your feelings instead of continuing the conversation. That's OK. That's resistance training. When their bad mood makes you angry, you're resisting their resistance. Resisting their resistance is like catching the flu; it's invisible and you don't know you got the bug until you start feeling really bad.

Physicians understand how draining it is to resist someone else's resistance. They see a patient who could by their own choices improve their health, but instead they want to keep smoking and eating junk food, and they want a pill to fix it all. Witnessing someone's resistance is difficult and takes a lot of energy when you care and want to fix it. But you can't fix other people, and the moment you take on their success more than they do, you're resisting their resistance. This isn't about not caring and leaving people to suffer. It's about requiring from others a sense of personal responsibility and self-empowerment. Certainly, it's a gray area where their resistance ends and your resistance to their resistance begins, but know this: when you want their success more than they do, or when you are trying too hard to create change, chances are you're resisting their resistance and doing the lion's share of their emotional work. This isn't to say that you let employees do anything they want or that you leave a hungry man starving to death in the desert. What this does mean is that you have choices when you're leading, and your choices are dependent upon their commitment to do their own work.

As a leader, you have to witness other people's resistance without getting sucked into their drama or swept away trying to make them happy. You can watch, observe, and strategize, but you can't and shouldn't want to change them. You can only offer them the choice to change. Using energy to change someone else is your resistance to their resistance, and this pattern is a prison for you and for them. Resisting their resistance is where most of us get hooked and can't get loose. The most insidious resistance is your resistance to their resistance.

The Fulcrum Point of Change

There is a place where change happens, and it's called willingness. Nothing happens until there is willingness. Resistance indicates a lack of willingness. Resistance drives managers and leaders crazy. As a leader, you want to quickly *test for resistance* on a regular basis. The more stuck the other person is, the more resistance you have to work through. Now review these phrases and try to figure out what they have in common:

➡ I would, but it takes too long.

➡ Yes, but I don't have the time.

➡ Don't blame me; you would feel the same way too.

➡ It's not my fault. It's because of _____ (fill in the blank).

As you noticed, all these phrases indicate resistance. Your goal as a leader is to get forward movement, but what so often happens is a game of verbal ping-pong where you wind up arguing about the irrelevant and unimportant. This is because while you were trying to get forward movement from a teammate, you reacted to their resistance and created yet another barrier. It goes like this:

Employee: "But it would take too long."

Leader: "Not really, all things considered."

Employee: "But I don't have the time."

Leader: "You just don't know how to prioritize. We all have the same twenty-four hours in each day."

Employee: "But it's expensive."

Leader: "Not when you consider how much you spend each day at the coffee shop on lattes."

None of these techniques ever move the needle. Instead, they become arguments, attachments, and distractions. When you resist someone else's resistance, you create more resistance, so the very first step for you as the leader is to be willing to hear their resistance and not offer back any resistance.

— Remove the Obstacle Using the Magic Phrase —

Suppose *I'm coaching you* to initiate a difficult conversation that you've been putting off. You have some resistance, but you're aware of your resistance, so you invite me to coach you out of resistance first.

Perhaps you say, "I already know what they'll say."

As your coach, I would ask you, "Are *you willing* to hear them anyway?"

If you say, "It's going to be difficult" . . .

Then, I will ask, "Are you *willing* to experience some difficulty?" Do you see how this works?

I'm listening for your barriers (real or perceived), and I don't argue with your reality. I'm not trying to change your mind. I'm just asking you if you are willing to overcome your barriers.

If you're willing to listen to the same old pattern and experience some difficulty to address an uncomfortable situation, then the needle has moved. You're no longer stuck, and you're no longer attached to what happens.

My focus here is on myself as your coach, not on what my client (you) will or won't do. I don't want to argue with you or convince you that I'm right. I just want to see if I can help you move the needle by testing for willingness. You can use this technique on a resistant employee. Here's what to do: first, overcome your own resistance to discomfort, stress, fear, or whatever is keeping you from taking action. Releasing your own resistance gives you the conflict capacity to work with their resistance. And . . . since you *already know* most of their patterns, you're prepared for what they might say. *Create space for their resistance.* When you simply allow their reaction, accepting them as they are, it changes the energy. When they resist by making excuses or blaming or showing signs of anger, *you* simply remain calm, simply listen, and acknowledge their reality. Then use the *magic phrase* "Are you willing?" or "Would you be willing?" I call this "overcoming the obstacle."

Employee: "But it's going to be difficult."

Leader: "Yes, it might be. Are you willing to do it anyway?"

Employee: "Well, the real issue is that it's time consuming."

Leader: "Yes, I hear you. It will take some time. Are you willing to allot the time?"

Employee: "I'm willing, but I don't know what Rhonda will think."

Leader: "I understand. Are you willing to move forward anyway?"

Let me give you a secret. The first objection someone has when in a state of resistance isn't usually the first barrier. The real obstacle is buried three or more deep. Keep using the magic phrase to unearth the real barrier.

Reduce the Obstacle

An alternative is to reduce the obstacle. The technique is to reduce the obstacle instead of asking them to completely overcome the obstacle. It goes like this:

Employee: "But it's going to be difficult."

Leader: "Yes, it might be, but if I could reduce the difficulty by 10 percent, would you be willing?"

Employee: "Well, the real issue is that it's time consuming."

Leader: "Yes, I hear you. If I could shave off ten hours, would you be willing?"

Employee: "I'm willing, but I don't know what Rhonda will think."

Leader: "I understand. What if I talk with Rhonda to get her agreement? Are you willing then?"

The Courage of Willingness

If you're afraid of getting your feelings hurt or being misunderstood, then you must be willing to have your feelings hurt or be misunderstood. If you're nervous about having to fire an employee who isn't stepping up to the plate, then you must be willing to let them go if they won't take coaching and direction. The fact is you can't have difficult conversations with employees when you're afraid of their response and you aren't willing to make tough calls. Before engaging in the conversation, you must get to a place of willingness instead of being attached to their agreement. Your state of willing-ness gives you a different energy when you speak, and they'll know that you care and you still mean business. If they pout, let them pout. If they get angry, it's OK as long as they don't hurt anyone. You don't return tit for tat, and you don't play games or use innuen-dos to make your point. You make your choices based on who you are, not on what everyone else is doing. You take on only what's yours to own just like Sherri B. did with Mr. Mason. The fulcrum point of change is where you *become willing* to move the needle. Willingness is the courage to feel uncomfortable, face your fears, and deal with the consequences. You'll discover you are so much stronger than you ever thought you were.

Reflection

1. What is a resistant pattern you see in another person?

2. How do you resist?

3. What must you be willing to do to change the pattern?

4. Which of the SAND patterns do you see most often?

7

Skills:
A Blueprint for
Difficult Conversations

The answers will come through the
conversation, not before the conversation.

atisha had been putting off a performance conversation with Janelle, her receptionist, for a couple of months. "Janelle is a good employee, and we love her, but lately her performance is slipping. She's constantly running to the restroom, or she's always checking her phone. It's not all her fault. These behaviors started when we were on partial lockdown for COVID and Janelle had to check on her kids. She was juggling a lot of balls, as we all were, but it hasn't improved, and I'm not quite sure where to start." This conversation was part of a facilitated general session at a state conference for healthcare administrators. Latisha had the courage to share with the group of one hundred participants what was first and foremost on her mind—where to start with a difficult conversation.

The previous day at this same conference, I heard several similar situations at a roundtable. Kendra, a veteran practice manager, said, "I used to start difficult conversations with a compliment, then work my way to talking about the problem, then end on a positive note. That's not working so well anymore. They know where I'm going after I give the first compliment." I told the roundtable group, "Consultants call these kinds of conversations a crap sandwich. You start and end with a slice of bread, but the middle is unpalatable." These difficult conversations sandwiched between compliments surprise employees and leave a bad taste in their mouths. When you say "We need to talk," they dread it and put up their defenses, and for good reason. No one likes to be blindsided. We all had a good laugh, and I invited them to my session the next morning. Another administrator summed it all up: "Sometimes you don't have anything good to say, and you just wish they'd go ahead and leave. It's just hard to know how to start, whether they are a great employee or one you want to let go."

This chapter is about initiating difficult conversations around performance and behaviors. We'll talk about how to preplan the conversation and how to set the right stage for the conversation. If you've ever played verbal ping-pong, this chapter will tell you how to stay on track and how to pick up on signs of resistance. If you've tried to talk to someone but your message didn't stick, you'll learn how to create accountability that feels supportive rather than punitive. We will work through the blueprint, and by the end, you will see how every skill works together in one singular conversation. You will also see along the way examples of how to use each skill on its own for small, stand-alone issues that don't require a longer conversation.

—— Why Difficult Conversations Are Difficult ——

Not knowing how to start a difficult conversation is one of the most common reasons for avoiding a conversation. Another reason for avoiding is simply because the difficult conversation might feel bad.

You avoid initiating the conversation because you don't want to hurt *their* feelings, but the truth is, you don't like how *you* feel when their feelings are hurt. You appease them because you don't want to make them defensive, but the truth is you don't like how *you feel* when they get defensive.

In the end, it's always about your own feelings. You don't like your own sarcastic thoughts. You don't like how you feel when someone resists your leadership. You worry that you might blow up. You don't trust yourself to stay calm. You're afraid you might take the bait and get distracted and end up in a completely different conversation than what you intended. It's not at all about them. It's all about you and what you don't want to feel, and that's how mismanagement begins.

Then one day something shifts. You realize that you're responsible only for how you behave and how you feel, and you don't want to project your insecurities on other people. You used to walk on eggshells protecting others. Looking back, you realize it's all a fib you told *yourself*. You weren't really protecting anyone else. You were protecting *you* from feeling things *you* didn't want to feel.

So, what do we do with feelings? Do we push them down? Do we deny them? No. Suppression only makes the situation worse. Whether it's aggression, avoidance, defensiveness, crying, pouting, withdrawing—we all handle feelings differently. Release your resistance by owning the truth, and stop judging yourself for being human. When you know where to start in a difficult conversation and how to lead the conversation, you can easily manage your internal conflict. If you have a blueprint for a conversation, with a set of skills that can be used as a process or used independently to clarify, gain understanding, or address conflict, difficult conversations become easier. With some practice, difficult conversations can even be exciting. That's because you're getting a rush of dopamine running through your system as you build new neuro-connections because of having learned something. You'll feel good, and you'll look forward to conversations, not because you enjoy catching people at their worst, but because through your conversations, you coach others to be at their best!

—————— Part 1: Leadership Clarity ——————

Start with leadership clarity. Before any conversation, get clear about three things: the situation at hand, your desired end result, and perceived obstacles. Refer back to chapter 3 for a quick review if necessary. In addition, get clear about how you want the conversation to go. Through your leadership clarity, you'll course correct any unwanted behaviors and substandard performance to align with business objectives. *This is the preparation phase* before you ever utter a word.

Be Specific about the Situation

1. What is happening that should not be happening?

2. What is not happening that should be happening?

3. How does this affect the business?

Most of us want to jump into problem-solving before getting a clear picture about what's happening or not happening. As a result, there's a lot of confusion about the current reality, and when you don't understand reality, you won't be clear about your pathway to success. Make friends with reality, and face the facts before assuming a conspiracy, a character flaw, or some ulterior motive. I'd be remiss if I didn't say that your understanding of current reality *may change* once you become engaged in the conversation, but I'm asking you to get *clear and specific about what's happening or not happening*. You will get better at this over time. You cannot solve a problem unless you get the situation right, and this process will help you get better at creating a situation analysis. With a lot of failed proposals in the beginning of my work as a consultant, I ultimately learned that if I can get the situation analysis right, I almost always close the contract.

It's imperative to know where you're starting, point A, and where you want to land, point B. What is point B? Is it a behavior change? Is it increasing sales by 30 percent? Is it reducing turnover? Is point B about acquiring a new skill or increasing productivity? Before you talk with your employee, you need to know what success looks like. We aren't really worried about the how right now. If you get "stuck on the rock called How," you are going to confuse yourself, and you'll get distracted in your conversation (see figure 6).

After you're clear, it's up to you to guide the conversation, create agreement, and create the structures of accountability. I can't say this enough: you aren't trying to problem-solve in the beginning. You're building a structure where the process or the how-to will be revealed later.

If you're stuck on how, you'll propose the wrong solution. You may ask your employee to take a course in project management, when in reality they just need to learn how to delegate. You may request a workshop for an entire group, when all you need is a one-on-one conversation between a director and a manager. What this means is that you must be willing to be in the unknown for a period of time during your prep work. *The answers will come through the conversation, not before the conversation. We are still in preparation mode here.*

The rock called How

FIGURE 6. The rock called How

Skill 1: Set the Intention

The very first skill before you ever utter a word in a live meeting is to craft a clear intention. The intention you craft in your office is the same intention you'll use in your in-person meeting. The reason to set your intention *prior to* the meeting is so that you don't fall onto an emotional land mine. An emotional land mine is when you think your intention is pure but you're still holding grudges and want revenge. I'll talk more about emotional land mines in a moment.

An intention is more powerful and more multifaceted than a goal. I think of intention as a goal with a soul. An intention considers the good of the organization as well as the good of the person you're coaching, the journey as well as the destination, the heart as well as the head. Goals are about outcomes. Intentions are also about outcomes, but an intention considers the question: What do I want this emotional experience to be? When you set an intention, you're essentially telling the other person what direction the conversation is going so they can let go of their worry and be present as you lead the conversation. Setting a proper intention provides direction and emotional safety. Remember that when you set your intention.

EXAMPLES OF GOOD INTENTION SETTING

→ My intention is to talk about how we can elevate your sales numbers.

→ My intention for this conversation is to discuss how we go forward after COVID.

→ My intention for this conversation is to explore ways to significantly improve teamwork.

→ My intention for this conversation is to talk about increasing accuracy on documentation.

EXAMPLES OF POOR INTENTION SETTING

➡ My intention is to find out why your sales are lagging.

➡ My intention for this conversation is to understand why you're making so many mistakes.

➡ My intention for this conversation is to talk about your bullying behavior.

➡ My intention for this conversation is to know why you aren't documenting.

When you set the intention, it is like you're saying, "Here's our north star. We are going forward, and if we get lost, we'll use this north star to course correct." There is magic in getting the intention right. Notice what works and doesn't work in the previous examples of good and poor intention setting: when the intention is well crafted, it's forward moving, it provides a sense of emotional safety, and it speaks to the desired end result. When the intention is crafted poorly, it speaks about the problem, sounds accusatory, is full of assumptions, and sounds punitive. If your conversations start to go south, it's either because you set the wrong intention or you didn't align to the intention you set. Be careful when crafting your intention. Don't yet focus on the how. The how will be revealed in the conversation. Make your focus positive instead of punitive. We are putting our focus on clarity, alignment, intention, and vision when we start the conversation. But what about bullying or aggressiveness, or lackluster performance? There's plenty of time later to bring forward what you've observed, specifically when it comes to bullying or other dysfunctional behaviors, but we must start with the vision first.

Emotional Land Mines

There's a land mine every leader must be aware of when setting an intention: emotions. You must clear your own emotional energy before actually speaking about your intention. If you're still holding a grudge, you won't be able to set a proper intention, and you put emotional safety at risk. This is part of emotional integrity and is an inner game you need to win. Refer back to chapter 4 if you need to review how to regain emotional regulation. If you feel angry because of their poor documentation or bullying behavior, then you're not ready to coach them from the purest intention. This is your work to do as a leader. Clean up any anger, resentment, or blame before you attempt to "help them"; otherwise, you're just fooling yourself and you're doing what every other mediocre leader does: documenting so that you can justify firing them. Remember, people do what they do because it has been allowed and they see no reason to change. If you've allowed the behavior for too long, you're probably angry with yourself. Own it and forgive yourself, and then you'll gain the courage to have this difficult conversation.

PRACTICE

My intention for this conversation is _____.

1. Does your intention have a north star quality?

2. Does your intention speak about the desired outcome?

3. Does your intention inspire or deflate?

Skill 2: State the Observed Behavior

This one skill will change the way you lead. Instead of making value judgments and assumptions, you use observed behavior to address dysfunctional behaviors and performance. Your objective is to understand the difference between the story you're telling yourself and the actual observable behavior. Look at the following matrix to see the difference.

Perception, assumption, generalization	Observed behavior
You have a bad attitude.	You have missed three deadlines this month.
She is rude and obnoxious.	She interrupts at meetings.
He isn't engaged.	He kept looking at his cell phone during our conversation.
They don't care.	When I asked if they would like to participate, they said, "I guess."

Notice how often we collapse language based on our own interpretations and judgments. The only way to understand another person is to bring forth observations and let them respond. They may disagree or defend, and that's OK, but they deserve to be heard.

Putting It Together

Suppose your first assumption is that Cliff has an attitude problem. You clean up your own perceptions and instead decide to talk with him in an honest way to address the elephant in the room, Cliff's behavior of eye-rolling. You envision the conversation going well, and being genuinely interested in getting the relationship back on track. You want to help Cliff, and you want to be a better leader and not let things go on for too long. In this case, you would use the skill of setting the intention and the skill of stating the observed behavior. In this scenario, use the first part of the blueprint and set an *appointment* with Cliff. When he arrives for your meeting, it would go like this:

> Cliff, the intention for this conversation is to talk about how we can increase engagement at meetings. What I've observed is that sometimes you cross your arms and roll your eyes. The story I'm telling myself is that you sometimes disagree, but you don't feel comfortable speaking in front of everyone else.

PRACTICE

My intention for this conversation is _____.

What I've observed is _____.

The story I'm telling myself is _____.

Then you would follow through with the rest of the conversation.

Although skill 2 is part of the blueprint, you can use this skill as a singular tool to correct unwanted perceptions or behaviors right in the moment, without the need for a longer conversation. For example, if Cliff lets out a sigh and rolls his eyes when you're making an announcement at a meeting, you immediately address the observed behavior by saying, "Cliff, do you disagree? Or is there something you want to say?" If this question catches Cliff off guard, he'll say, "No, I'm fine." However, the very fact that you noticed and inquired will change Cliff's behaviors about 75 percent of the time. If not, you can grab Cliff when you see him in the hallway and revisit. "Cliff, when I was speaking earlier, I noticed that you crossed your arms, and I thought you rolled your eyes. The story I'm telling myself is that you disagree, or you have something important to say that you haven't yet said."

Then take a pregnant pause. If Cliff is honest, this is the time for him to come forth and discuss the subject at hand. Notice the technique here: speak about the observed behavior in terms of "What I noticed" or "I observed . . . ," and then add your own take on it: "The story I'm telling myself is . . ." or "What I perceived was . . ." This works because you're being vulnerable enough to share your interpretations. This kind of honesty without judgment is severely shocking to most people. Why? Because we allow too many elephants into the room. We notice Cliff's eye-rolling, but we won't give him the "satisfaction" of knowing that we know. Then we get resentful and say something sarcastic, and he strikes back with an innuendo or arrives late to a meeting, and the game continues because no one has the courage to bring the elephant into the room. Here's another example: You hear sarcasm in Ramon's voice at a board meeting. Say, "I noticed that when you don't agree, you say, 'Well, that's original,' and it sounds like there's a hidden meaning there." A pregnant pause or a simple "What's going on with that?" will open a conversation at best or at least let your colleague know you aren't going to ignore inappropriate behavior. This technique gives them a chance to course correct without having to have a longer conversation because the problem has gone on for too long.

Skill 3: Speak to the Vision

Most of the time we focus on the shark instead of on the island, the obstacle instead of the goal. When we speak to the vision (the intended outcome), we focus more on what we want and less on what we don't want. In the previous example (picking on poor Cliff again), you wouldn't say, "Look, Cliff, I don't want you to keep rolling your eyes and crossing your arms." You would say, "What I want is to have an open dialogue when you disagree." You wouldn't say, "Look, I don't want to criticize you." Instead, you'd say, "I want to help you communicate more effectively in your role."

Look at the grid once again to see the difference.

What I don't want	What I do want
I don't want to argue.	I want to find agreement.
I don't want to hurt your feelings.	I want to help you grow.
I don't want you to be a bully.	I want you to be supportive of the team.
I don't want to micromanage.	I want you to take initiative.
I don't want to hear your negativity.	I want to hear your ideas and solutions.

Since most of us alternately speak in terms of what we don't want and what we do want, here's a way to balance the two. Anytime you hear yourself saying, "I don't want . . . ," finish your sentence, and then circle back and say, "What I do want . . ." This clarifies your end result and is more direct and to the point. I often use "What I want" and "What I don't want" together. I'll say something like, "I want to help you. What I don't want is to have you think you're taking the blame." Or, if I catch myself starting with what I don't want, it may sound like this: "I don't want to make a big deal out of this . . . what I do want is for us to make it simple so we have a better system in the future."

PRACTICE

I don't want _____.
What I do want is _____.

Putting It Together

Cliff, **the intention** for this conversation is to talk about how we can increase engagement at meetings. **What I've observed** is that sometimes you cross your arms and roll your eyes. The story I'm telling myself is that you sometimes disagree, but you don't feel comfortable speaking in front of everyone else. **What I don't want** is to catch you off guard again at a meeting. **What I want** is to create better and more open conversation.

In this scenario, I showed an example of catching yourself if you start to go down the road of "What I don't want" and quickly course correcting to talk about the outcome you do want. It helps to know you're going to speak about what you want *in addition to* what you don't want, but the most important piece here is to speak to the vision, which is speaking to exactly what you want.

Skill 4: Make a Business Case

So why does it matter that Cliff rolls his eyes, or that Jada doesn't document correctly, or that Amari constantly runs late? If it's only because it irritates you, then it's not a good enough reason to spend energy on a conversation. In these cases, it's just a personality issue and an indication that perhaps you need to stretch to allow for differences. Most likely that's not the reason for your distress. The reason to address an issue is because the behavior or the performance affects the business. This is the piece so often missing when it comes to addressing performance or behavior; we haven't established the impact of the problem on the business; therefore, employees just think you're nitpicking. Here are some easy examples:

- → The mistake affects patient safety.
- → The behavior promotes a toxic work environment.
- → The tardiness reduces sales opportunities.
- → The improper attire tarnishes our hard-earned brand.
- → This behavior reduces departmental trust.
- → This behavior is affecting our sales.
- → This issue is resulting in lost customers.
- → This habit is affecting our ability to fulfill orders.
- → This threatens patient safety.
- → This inaccurate documentation sets us up for a possible lawsuit.

Business Objectives

Think in terms of people, productivity, and profits. Make a short list of five or six business objectives that are a priority in your culture.

- → Patients, customers, clients
- → Profits, revenues, sales
- → Productivity, teamwork, collaboration

→ Brand, reputation, loyalty

→ Risk, safety, compliance

PRACTICE

Think of a performance problem or a behavioral issue. Now determine how it affects one of your business objectives. Think in terms of clients, patients, customers, revenue, sales, productivity. This problem affects _____.

Putting It Together

Cliff, **the intention** for this conversation is to talk about how we can increase engagement at meetings. **What I've observed** is that sometimes you cross your arms and roll your eyes. The story I'm telling myself is that you sometimes disagree, but you don't feel comfortable speaking in front of everyone else. **What I don't want** is to catch you off guard again at a meeting. **What I want** is to create better and more open conversation. This behavior **affects engagement** at important team meetings and makes others afraid to speak up as well.

Checking Your Conflict Resistance

Obviously, these skills look doable when you're reading about Cliff, Jada, Kim, and other people you don't know. Everyone knows the answers when they're in the workshop or when they are reading about it. The real test comes when you're confronted with a situation that makes your heart beat a little faster—when you worry that you'll do it wrong, be misunderstood, or make someone angry. So, the real question here is, Are you willing? If you keep coming up with excuses, go back and read the chapter on releasing resistance. The only way to move the needle is for you as a leader to be willing.

This doesn't mean you'll do it right the first time or that it won't feel uncomfortable. It will. But your willingness is the fulcrum point that will change your leadership. The first part of this blueprint is to gain leadership clarity. We've done that. Here's the checklist so you can see the process at one glance. The first list represents your preparation before the actual conversation, and the checklist that follows represents the order in which you speak once the meeting is initiated. With that said, I recommend using every bullet including the checklist to prepare for the meeting until you have mastered the process and can do it by memory.

PART 1: LEADERSHIP CLARITY

Prepare for your conversation in advance of initiating the conversation.

→ Describe point A, the current reality.

→ Define point B, the end result.

→ Set a meeting date.

→ Set the intention (preconversation).

THE CONVERSATION

✓ The intention for this conversation
✓ What I've observed
✓ What I want
✓ What I don't want
✓ How this affects the business

Now you know how to start, but once you have gone through the checklist and have talked about how the problem affects the business, how do you stay in charge of the conversation? How do you avoid getting distracted by the employee and ending up in a completely different conversation? For the second part of the conversation, you need to stay present to the unknown, trust the process, and facilitate employee clarity. You do that through staying focused on the blueprint and discerning what's really going on.

Part 2: Employee Clarity

Now it's time to have the most interesting part of the conversation—the part where it's easy to get derailed and lose your cool. If you've ever wondered, "How did I get here?" this part will help you stay in charge of the conversation even though you aren't talking that much. The first skill is to think like a consultant and to try to understand what's going on in your employee's experience.

Skill 5: Get Curious

Very few people are curious these days. To be curious you have to believe that there might be a juicy nugget missing, or some hidden agenda or a piece of information that gives you the power of clarity. You can't be a know-it-all. You can't be the type of leader who believes every assumption that pops into your mind. You must be willing to be wrong, be willing to be surprised. Curiosity is a fun skill to cultivate, and it changes the conversation. The first part of the conversation sounds like this: "My intention for this conversation is to talk about getting your documentation up to date. I've noticed that for the last three weeks there's been no documentation. The story I'm telling myself is that you no longer think it's important, but this puts us at risk for making costly mistakes in customer service." Next, ask a focused question related to the issue at hand. It goes like this:

➡ Walk me through your thought process.

➡ Help me understand what's happening?

➡ I'm curious, what changed over the last three weeks?

You'll need to listen objectively when you get to this part of the conversation. You can't allow yourself to get drawn into excuses, blame, or distractions. You'll have to think like a consultant, be objective, avoid distractions, and get to the root of the problem.

Skill 6: Think like a Consultant

Your employee gets to talk now. They will tell you stories. They will share emotions. They may cry or get angry. Your goal is to listen for clues. There's a reason for the performance problem, and there's a reason for bad behavior. You aren't assuming or judging, just listening to uncover the root problem. You'll find your answer in one of these five categories:

1. Clarity

2. Skill

3. Priorities

4. Resources

5. Willingness

Listen for clues that there has been a lack of clarity. If you've been inconsistent, you'll find out in this conversation. If the rules aren't being adhered to or something isn't fair, this conversation will expose that to you. Clarity issues will also be found in the other four categories, so stay attentive to these categories.

Next listen for skills issues. It's easy to miss skills issues, but so often the issue is related to a skills deficit. I've seen VPs that on the surface looked competent but couldn't project manage. I've seen directors who couldn't delegate and instead micromanaged. I've seen C-suite leaders who were afraid of bad news and didn't know how to separate their feelings from the facts. I've seen account managers who didn't know how to use a calendar; therefore, they missed sales calls. Warning: It's easy to get angry and make up a story about them not caring, needing an attitude adjustment, or working the system. Avoid these stories yourself and figure out what skill is missing. Maybe you assumed because of their résumé that they should know how to do something, but ask yourself if your organization offered onboarding and training or if there has ever been feedback and coaching on the issue at hand. Did you assume competency because of confidence?

If it's not a skills issue, see if the priorities are crystal clear. There are certain leaders who are so visionary and so future focused that they keep shifting priorities, keeping everyone's heads spinning. It's frustrating for the employees who are trying to get to the island but the map keeps changing. This is both a priority issue and a leadership and clarity issue at the core, and not about the employee. Priority issues are common in startups, government agencies, and entrepreneurial, fast-growth companies.

Could the issue be resources? It might seem like a resource issue on the surface when the employee is simply not resourceful or doesn't take initiative. Get real about what resources are needed to complete the job without undue stress, and if you simply can't get the resources, find innovative ways to encourage resourcefulness. I've worked with franchisees who had employees with babysitting issues or broken-down cars as their reasons for tardiness. While the facts are there, with a little coaching and planning, these employees learned how to plan for emergencies or find ways to do some of their work from home.

Another note about resources: Sometimes we humans go through traumatic experiences such as the death of a loved one, a divorce, or an illness. We have to understand, when it comes to resources, an individual's *personal resources* might be tapped out, and they are at capacity. This is where you help problem-solve and get them the help they need, whether it's paid time off, access to mental health, or some other way to support them at a difficult time.

You can't fix these kinds of problems if the filter you're looking through is about their character or lack of engagement. At various levels, depending on the type of job, some employees just need some mentoring and encouragement to help them become empowered so they can rise to the next level. Here are some examples of conversations and how they relate to the five categories:

Kayla comes in at nine on Wednesdays, so I thought it was OK.	Clarity
I haven't spoken to him because I'm afraid he won't take it well, and I can't afford to lose him right now.	Skill
You said the most important thing was that I get the report done; that's why I didn't make the sales introduction.	Priority
My computer broke down.	Resources or resourcefulness
I would, but it would take too much time.	Priority or willingness

When you listen to your employee explaining why things aren't going well, listen for these five categories of clarity, skill, priority, resources, and willingness. Stop taking things personally and instead see yourself more as an investigative reporter trying to find the key that unlocks the mystery. You can fix almost any other problem with skills training, objectives clarification, prioritization, better communication, and the right resources. What you can't overcome is a resistant employee who fails to take responsibility, has a fixed mindset, and is unwilling to learn. At some point in this conversation, you'll know what the issue is. Using the grid as an example, if the computer broke down, it's an issue of resources, and if the employee thought the report was needed immediately, it took priority over making a sale. These issues are easy to course correct, and as their leader, you're going to ask them to do something to change their behavior. This is when the conversation reveals resistance and requires the skill of radical listening.

Skill 7: Radical Listening

Here's what to expect when you get to this point. As you open up the conversation to your employees, they may tell you some stories about what's happening, why it's not fair, and what their obstacles are, and they might even blame you for not understanding. Don't get pulled in. Listen, but listen objectively. Radical listening is about the ability to listen even when it's extremely difficult, when every bone in your body wants to explain, lecture, defend, or make wrong. This takes a lot of self-discipline and courage. You'll need to put the tip of your tongue on the roof of your mouth to listen better. Stop interrupting, tempting as it may be. Practice saying, "I see" and "I didn't know you felt that way" and "I hear you" and, most of all, "That sounds frustrating" or "It sounds like you're angry." It goes like this:

> Employee: "It's so difficult to do what you're asking me to do."
>
> You: "I didn't know you felt that way."
>
> Employee: "Well, it's not like everyone else is required to do what you're asking."
>
> You: "It sounds like it's really frustrating to you."
>
> Employee: "No, I'm just a little angry."
>
> You: "You're angry?"
>
> Employee: "Yes, and scared that I won't be able to be successful."
>
> You: "I hear you. Are you open to some ideas and some coaching?"
>
> Employee: "Yes."

What you *don't want to do* is take the bait and get into a conversation of verbal ping-pong:

> Employee: "It's so difficult to do what you're asking me to do."

You: "Look, it's part of your job."

Employee: "Well, it's not like everyone else is required to do what you're asking."

You: "They are at a different pay scale. You knew that when you took this job!"

Employee: "You just don't understand, and it's not fair."

You: "If you don't like it, you can take a pay cut or find another place to work."

Employee: "Never mind. I'll try."

You: "OK. Good luck."

In the second scenario, do you think you moved the needle or caused even more resentment? Chances are, that employee will huddle up with other teammates and gossip. The point here is you might have encouraged compliance but not commitment. Your goal is not to win an argument. Your goal is to make your employee feel heard so you can break through. If they perceive that you're lecturing, judging, or waiting to document them, you won't get to the truth, they won't improve, and you'll have to let them go and search for a new employee.

Listen for subtle clues of resistance or lack of confidence. For example, when you're coaching an employee to do something bold and they say, "I'll try . . . ," don't say, "Great!" and think it's done. There's a subtle clue in "I'll try," which means they aren't confident, or they aren't committed. This can trigger you if you aren't careful. Don't use the tired old saying "There is no such thing as *try!*" Instead, you say something like, "It sounds like you aren't confident you can achieve this goal?" Either they'll consider their language or it will open a dialogue about their perceived barriers, to which you can then offer mentoring, advice, or coaching. See the difference curiosity makes in the quality of the conversation? You go from quoting Yoda to understanding what's behind someone's language. If you keep hearing issues of being stuck, attached, negative, or distracted (SAND), then you can test for resistance using the magic phrase. The important piece up to this point is that you manage your own resistance.

Skill 8: The Magic Phrase

Remember the magic phrase we introduced in chapter 6: "Would you be willing . . . ?" Your goal isn't to win an argument or play "gotcha." Please don't assume they aren't willing. You are only *testing for* willingness here. What I've learned in over two decades is the first barrier is usually a pseudobarrier. The real issue is buried about three layers deep. The method is to dissolve the resistance through agreement, and then use the magic phrase to test for willingness. It goes like this:

> *Employee: "But it seems really difficult."*
>
> *You: "Yes, it might be difficult. Are you willing to try?"*
>
> *Employee: "Well, it's really not that difficult; it's just time consuming."*
>
> *You: "Yes, it might be time consuming. Are you willing to do it?"*
>
> *Employee: "I might look stupid when I try it the first time."*
>
> *You: "Yes, you might feel stupid. Are you willing to go for it anyway?"*

In this example, there were three layers of resistance, or three barriers, if you will: difficulty, time consumption, and feeling stupid. Chances are the real issue is about self-image or being judged by others. You would have never uncovered that if you had played ping-pong:

> *Employee: "But it seems difficult."*
>
> *You: "Oh, come on now, you've done difficult things before."*

Employee: "Well, this is even more difficult than before."

You: "You can do it! I know you can. You are one of our best sales reps."

Employee: "I'm not sure . . ."

You: "You just need to work on your self-confidence."

When someone resists your efforts, the first impulse is to argue or persuade. Sometimes you think you're helping, but usually you're causing more resistance by arguing. There's a time to be a cheerleader and a time to test for resistance. With this method, you aren't offering any counterresistance. There's absolutely no push-pull to your agenda. *Objections die on agreement.* If you can meet people where they are and agree with their view of the world, you can use the magic phrase to uncover the perceived barriers.

Let's circle back to the five categories we listed before: clarity, priorities, resources, skills, and willingness. Suppose you have asked them to be willing to do something to improve. Perhaps it's a request to take a course to up-level their skills, or maybe you've asked them to shift priorities. Let's assume they are willing. It will feel good that you have come this far in the conversation, but don't make the most fatal mistake: failure to set agreement and accountability.

Skill 9: Getting Agreement and Accountability

I can't tell you how many times I've had a leader say, "I spoke with them, and they improved for a while, but now they're back to old habits." This is probably due to a lack of accountability. Everyone felt good after the drama of a difficult conversation, and there's a glow you feel after resolving an intense argument. Don't let this happen. The next step is to get their agreement to meet again in two weeks to check on progress. Explain how you'll measure progress and what you expect to happen in two weeks. Get their agreement that you'll coach them if you see anything not measuring up.

Then promptly put your accountability conversation on the calendar and send an invite. In two weeks, you'll review their progress and uncover possibly more barriers. You'll test for additional levels of resistance, and you'll encourage them for the gains they've made. Set another accountability meeting; this time choose two weeks, three weeks, or a month, depending on the complexity of the situation and their progress.

I'm betting that if I were to quiz you about this process, you'd pass with flying colors. If we were in a workshop together, you'd get the answers right. If you're studying this model with a colleague, you'd be able to advise them effectively. Perhaps you've highlighted and dog-eared this information so that when the time comes, you'll be ready; however, using this model effectively comes down to practice. In the real world, you'll mess up, feel scared, get distracted, play verbal ping-pong, and wonder why these techniques didn't work. A gentle reminder: Be kind to yourself. Skill building takes willingness, practice, and courage. Everyone knows the answer in a workshop or after reading a book. Real skills development doesn't happen from reading a book or attending a workshop. It comes from real-life practice.

Once these practices become habits, you'll save time and see business results. By the second conversation, if you don't see improvement, the employee usually self-selects to leave, and it's peaceful and cooperative. Once you get good at this, you have fewer of these long, drawn-out conversations and instead you use the skills as needed while improving your relationships, the trust levels, and the quality of your conversations with your teammates.

Reflection

1. How does good intention setting create emotional safety?

2. What is the preparation you need before initiating your next conversation?

3. Who do you need to have a conversation with? How will you use this blueprint?

4. What resistance do you think you'll see in your next conversation? Is it within yourself or the other person?

8

Responsibility:
The Recognition of Choice

When you find your choice, you find your power.

Lana was exhausted from sorting through her business partner Jim's nasty emails in all caps. Fear became a constant companion to Lana, who avoided, appeased, and walked on eggshells trying to manage Jim. This management style took a toll on Lana's health and well-being. As a business partner, Jim was self-destructive, often threatening to withhold resources Lana needed to fulfill business agreements. Several times a month, Lana took to her bed with a stress headache, and her productivity plummeted. Even with coaching, Lana was unable to make any significant gains. The only thing on Lana's mind was how to control Jim. She wasn't interested in initiating a difficult conversation, setting a boundary, or managing her own stress. She was obsessed with Jim—what Jim said, what Jim did, and what Jim might do in the future. It's difficult to work with a bully, especially when the bully is your business partner, financially tied to your business.

Lana had choices, but she couldn't see them. When I suggested buying Jim's shares so she could take ownership, she quickly dismissed the idea. Even though Jim was making unilateral and illegal decisions, Lana refused to consider taking legal action. When we discussed setting boundaries, that wasn't an option because Lana was too afraid of retaliation. Because Lana couldn't see her choices, she couldn't take responsibility. All she could do is blame Jim and see herself as powerless. Lana was on the hamster wheel of indecision—a prisoner of her own business. In Lana's own words, she had "no other choice but to stick it out."

Whether you're a partner in a business, an executive in a Fortune 500, or a manager in a small enterprise, every organization has a "Jim." These individuals are often powerful, aggressive, combative, and unreasonable. Most people walk on eggshells to avoid those they experience to be aggressive, high-conflict people because they would rather change Jim than expand their comfort zone. If there's a Jim in your life, here's my advice: Stop trying to change Jim. He won't budge. Instead, you must focus on winning the inner game by accessing a different kind of power.

This chapter is about the dynamics of power, choice, and responsibility and why it's important to develop the skill of recognizing choice in any situation. We'll explore the balance between choice and responsibility and how leaders can use this balance in decision-making. If there is unresolved conflict related to decision-making, this chapter gives you a snapshot of how decision-making and choice either contribute to or reduce disruptive conflict.

The Power of Choice

You can't *make a choice* when you can't see the choices available. When you believe you have no choices, you become a prisoner of what other people do or don't do—a victim of circumstance.

Many conflicts would end if we could recognize the power of choice. How often do we make life and business decisions from the belief that there are no other choices? I have no choice but to stay in this job. I have no choice but to leave. I have no choice but to put up with their behavior because they are a top performer. I have no choice but to feel the way I feel. I have no choice but to act the way I act. I have no choice given my background, race, gender, history, experience. It doesn't matter what the context, when you fail to see your choices, or believe there are no choices, you unconsciously take on a victim mentality and see yourself as powerless. If you're in a pattern like Lana and Jim, you owe it to yourself and to those you lead to clean up any area where you portray yourself as one who has no choices.

───── Change Your Narrative about Choice ─────

Before you lead others, you have to lead yourself. You must become the example of choice abundance instead of choice scarcity. Stop talking about having no choices. Anytime you feel conflicted about what to do with your business partner, employee, director, or work culture, remind yourself that you have choices, even if you don't see them yet. Don't believe the narrative that your well-being is dependent on outside circumstances—that you need someone to change in order to be happy, productive, or fulfilled. Most of these ideas about powerlessness are an illusion. There will always be challenges, and there will always be people who are difficult to work with, but if you always see your choices, this isn't a big problem, only an opportunity to exercise your power of choice. No matter what you've been through, stop talking about your lack of choice. Instead say, "My best choice here is . . ." Or if you really don't have any viable choices, simply say, "Given the circumstances, the best choice was to . . ." Know that you made the best choice for you at the time.

Suppose you were done wrong: you've been dismissed, been discounted, been talked down to, had the opportunity taken from you, or been done wrong on a business deal. What if someone couldn't see your potential because of their own bias—their ego, or their ulterior motives?

Let's face it, the business world can be eye-opening—even cruel. You may be deceived, skipped over for a promotion, and not recognized for your efforts. In the world at large, there are self-serving and unconscious people who create intentional acts of harm toward others because of their beliefs, religion, race, or gender. There are plenty of instances where someone was truly victimized by a situation, a person, or a group of people, and we should seek justice for those harmed. Those who intentionally violate another should be held accountable. At the same time, whether the offense was large or small, whether you have been simply overlooked or intentionally victimized, life will go on. It's your choice how to identify. Don't rip yourself off by identifying as a victim.

To adopt this philosophy of personal responsibility and choice, you must entertain the both-and mindset rather than the either-or mindset. You were discounted, but you don't have to identify with having no worth. The event (harassment, abuse, attack) happened, but you don't have to create a lifetime identity of seeing yourself as a victim. This philosophy may sound harsh to some people, especially those who have been *wronged* by a person, group, or circumstance, but give me a chance to explain. The greatest disservice we can do to ourselves is to view ourselves as a victim. While we might have been *mistreated* for any number of reasons, to adopt the *identity* of victimhood is to agree to a life of imprisonment. That imprisonment is only in the mind. The narrative keeps the story alive, and we fail to see the choices to reinvent, realign, and facilitate real change. If you identify with victimhood, your brain looks for evidence that people are against you, and you'll continue to see evidence that you aren't considered or included. If you have been traumatized and can't get over what happened years ago, seek support in the form of therapy, coaching, or counseling. You owe it to yourself to focus on the future instead of being bound by a past incident. You have to trust yourself to move forward and not make your decisions based on a fear that someone or some group is out to get you.

If you see yourself as empowered, you'll make empowered choices that align with a vision of your future. Even in less than satisfactory circumstances, when you see yourself as having choices, you'll ask for what you want, set boundaries, and engage in the process of building your own strength and leadership identity. Your new vision of yourself will attract into your life people and opportunities that align with who you really are.

Reclaiming Power

Disappointments happen to all of us no matter what our role, title, or tenure, but no matter what happens, we always have a choice to leave unsatisfactory conditions. Dilan, a director of a manufacturing plant, was supposed to take over the GM position once his boss Howard retired; however, Howard only retired on paper. Howard was in the office every single day acting as if he were still in charge. To top it off, Howard visited the office daily to visit with Roberta, the office manager, who just happened to be his daughter. Dilan patiently waited it out, and eventually Howard stopped his daily office visits. Even so, Roberta had the final say because she had the owner's ear since her dad Howard was the owner's best friend. This interconnection of a family-owned business with tenured employees created an impossible culture for Dilan to make leadership decisions.

"When Roberta and I had differing opinions about production and maintenance decisions, she ruled by proxy, even though these areas were out of her wheelhouse." Dilan realized he was between a rock and a hard place, but he refused to see himself as a victim. He left for another job. When Dilan got an offer at a new company with a forty-thousand-dollar pay increase, it was a no-brainer. In this example, we see many of the issues we've already covered. There's a lack of clarity about roles and responsibilities, identity issues, and internal environment (culture) issues preventing forward movement. In addition, Dilan was expending too much energy in resistance to be happy and productive in his new role. In short, there was an imbalance of power and responsibility, and Dilan was in a no-win situation. Dilan didn't spend time trying to convince the owner to change the culture, and he didn't get into power struggles or resistance with the previous general manager or the office manager. Not one to be victimized by the culture, Dilan got the clarity he needed and then landed a better job. He left without the residue of resentment or the burden of seeing his former company as a persecutor, instead seeing it as a catalyst for positive change based on his own power of choice. The message here is about choice, personal responsibility, and empowerment. We must lead by example if we want to grow responsible employees.

Growing Responsible Employees

As a leader, you deal on an ongoing basis with employees who see themselves as having no choice. It's easy to dismiss or ignore these employees because they drain your energy. The most powerful action you can take is to help employees become empowered by seeing their choices. After you become more responsible yourself and consciously work to eliminate reactive language, you'll start to notice the red flags that indicate a lack of responsibility among employees: blaming, obsessing about the past, using disrespectful language, making excuses, or saying "I don't have any choices." If you aren't paying attention, old patterns will creep in and you'll be mesmerized by the story and start overcompensating for them or allowing less than they are capable of.

When you're leading others, it's important to discern between the facts of a situation and the other person's experience of the situation. The way people view themselves (their identity) comes out in their language. Their language and behaviors indicate victimhood or empowerment. So, listen and be empathetic, but challenge them to be all they can be and help them see their choices in any given moment. In addition, consciously seek ways to shape the environment to open up new networks of cooperation and trust that will enable them to trust their power of choice instead of always relying on an authority to tell them what to do or not do. This may come through mentoring, coaching, personal development opportunities, or focus groups where you listen to their experiences.

The way you view your employees (or anyone, for that matter) is paramount to their growth. Don't rip off your employees by viewing them as needy or helpless, even when they speak or act that way. Instead, see them as a powerful creator who has failed to recognize their choices. When you feel sorry for an employee, you're seeing them as powerless. When you allow behavior and feel you need to rescue them, you're seeing them as helpless. When you avoid a conversation because you believe they're too weak, you're seeing them as incapable. *If you make agreement with victimhood, you create victims!* Your employees will be overly dependent upon you, and they won't believe in themselves. Be intentional about how you see others. See their gifts. See their potential. See them as having agency, and support them in seeing their choices.

It's helpful that you understand this concept: when you find your choice, you find your power. This understanding saves hours of listening to complaints that can't be resolved, arguments that can't be won, and gossip about whose fault it is. You'll grow responsible employees, not dependent individuals who need you to fix things for them. When we don't recognize our choices, we become addicted to programmed, unconscious patterns of thought and behavior that keep us from growing. The first requirement of responsibility is the recognition of choice. You can't choose something you don't know is there.

Consider the parable of the beggar sitting on an old dirty chest filled with gold. The riches are there, but they don't see their choice, so they continue day after day seeking help from others. I was that beggar when I felt stuck in a job I had outgrown and thought there was no other choice. You are that beggar when you feel trapped in a business relationship that tests your integrity and takes a toll on your health. Your employee is that beggar when they keep coming to you and you keep covering for them versus helping them see their own treasures.

As leaders, we need to understand how detrimental it is to make agreement with powerlessness. We inspire others when we recognize our choices and encourage others to see their choices. When we know we have choices, we stop sitting on the chest of gold looking outside of ourselves for the rescue. If the system needs to be fixed, we realize that we can't wait for the system to change. We are the system. We must be the change. When we finally get it, we find our own gold and we help others find their gold.

——— Stop Advising and Start Coaching ———

Leaders make several mistakes when helping employees discover their choices. One mistake is giving advice too soon. Coaching isn't advice giving. Coaching is asking questions. Instead of saying, "Well, as I see it, you have three choices . . . ," say instead, "Have you looked at all of your choices?" or "What choices have you considered?" Your goal is to bypass your need to show how smart you are and allow your employee the space to process their concerns and figure it out on their own.

I'll admit, it's tempting to blurt out the answer, but you need to hold back. You must become disciplined at watching their answers unfold instead of ruining the surprise. Meet them where they are. Don't rush ahead and get too excited. The real thrill comes when you see their innovative spirit and increased confidence. The way you'll know you rushed through is by the level of resistance they offer back. If you find yourself arguing your case, you've gone too far. This is a delicate balance of knowing the answer but not giving it away and instead asking the questions they need to see the light. When you want their change more than they do, you'll overstep your bounds, and they'll resist all the "choices" you give them.

When you tell someone what to do, they tell you why it won't work and why you're wrong. Here's a warning: you'll be angry if you invest lots of time listening to complaining only to give advice that wasn't accepted. You'll feel disrespected. Don't get entwined in their problems, and don't get distracted spending time on what's not possible. If they have an audience or an ear, they'll gladly talk more about their sharks than their island. Your job is to keep them focused on what they want (the island) and to ask them about what kind of choices they have considered to get them there. When an individual figures out their own solution, they become engaged and committed. When they find their choice, they've found their power.

When you work with an employee who's blaming, don't take the bait. Instead ask, "What did you learn?" Ask them, "What choice do you have now?" When you hear "I don't have any choices," don't get mesmerized by the story and fly in for the rescue. Instead coach that employee to own the power they have: their own choices in the matter. Until the employee sees their choices, they are operating from a victim mentality and losing the inner game. They become suggestible to the little voice that tells them the system is rigged, there's no way to win, and there's really no choice but to resort to violence, steal from the company, or do something detrimental to their own future. Choices may exist, but if they don't see them, they become a prisoner to their own negative mindset, and this negative mindset creates an inner conflict that manifests into conflict with the system, bosses, colleagues, and coworkers.

The Balance between Choice and Responsibility

Anytime you hear someone say, "There are no choices," your antenna should go up warning you that the lack of responsibility follows absence of choice. When people don't see their choices, they abdicate responsibility. Here's why: responsibility is about ownership. When we don't take ownership, it means someone had to force us through "accountability" or some sort of punishment. People who feel forced to do something cast blame; after all, there was "no choice" but to follow orders. People who own their choices also own their results.

Where there are unresolved conflicts, look at the balance between choice and responsibility, and you'll find that either there's too much choice and not enough responsibility or too much responsibility and not enough choice. Think of a teeter-totter with balancing weights on each end, where when perfectly balanced, the teeter-totter is parallel to the ground (see figure 7).

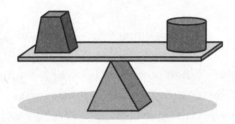

FIGURE 7. Balance between choice and responsibility

On the left side is responsibility, and on the right side is choice. Choice and responsibility need to be proportionate to balance the teeter-totter. If there's too much choice and not enough responsibility, there's an imbalance, and vice versa (see figure 8). To put this in practical terms, when a leader is given too much responsibility but not the authority (choice) to enforce their decisions, imbalance and unresolvable conflict follow. Let me share a couple of examples to make this concept practical.

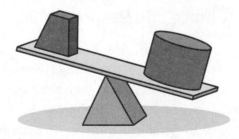

FIGURE 8. Lack of balance between responsibility and choice

Randall was hired as a security manager for a city government office and was tasked with taking on a change agent role for a particular department where there was a lot of workplace drama and lack of trust. Randall was hired to fix these departmental problems, build trust, and help employees work collaboratively. Randall discovered that one of his employees, Paulette, couldn't get along with her coworkers. She had been accused of being abrasive. She used derogatory language, often erupted in emotional outbursts, and had even physically assaulted a coworker. When Randall tried to discipline Paulette, he wasn't backed up by the city council. It appeared to him that Paulette was untouchable. First, the organization was unionized. Second, Paulette had seniority and had been an employee for over fifteen years. Third, Paulette had lost one of her children in a tragic accident several years ago. Top decision-makers felt sorry for Paulette, and they justified her behavior. To top it off, Paulette often brought in lunch or desserts for all the council members and had endeared herself to those at the top. Randall had the responsibility for the department but was metaphorically handcuffed and didn't have enough authority (choice) to make a difference. Needless to say, Randall left the organization and found employment elsewhere, as did Dilan, whom we talked about earlier.

Think deeply about the balance between choice (freedom and power) and responsibility. With more choice comes more responsibility. With more responsibility comes greater freedom and choice. A business owner has more responsibilities than their managers, but they also have the freedom (choice) to close the business, expand, or change locations. Frontline workers don't have as many choices (freedom or power) about how to use their time as do their managers, but their managers also have more responsibility. At the appropriate age, an individual gets the choice to drive, but the freedom doesn't come without responsibility attached—a driver's license and adherence to the law. Abuse the responsibility and lose the choice. More choices mean more responsibility. More responsibly means expanded choice. There's always a balance between choice and responsibility.

———————— Decision-Making and Power ————————

Power struggles often occur in corporate settings because the power is not assigned appropriately, or because there isn't a good decision-making process that supports responsible choice. Decisions and choices that should be based on expertise are instead based on some other arbitrary measure, such as longevity, seniority, or being a member of a union. Here's an example from a physician friend of mine, Michelle, who shared her experience of being undermined by a frontline employee:

> In the urgent care setting where doctors rotate on 12-hour shifts, I once was undermined by a front desk receptionist. I gave my patient a prescribed number of days off, but the receptionist interrupted and corrected me saying their office only allows two days off. This is a physician's decision, not a receptionist's decision nor is it a corporate decision. A few hours later, her work buddy on the clinical side refused to assist me. I was a temp doctor at that time and was hired through an agency. That was quite some time ago, and I was not sent back to that facility, yet they were in the wrong, not me.

We'll never know the reasons the receptionist didn't understand proper protocol, but lack of clarity often contributes to unnecessary conflict. The receptionist thought she had the power to override the physician, and the physician clearly knew that her expertise determined the power of decision-making. Now there's a conflict due to a disagreement of who's in charge and what the rules are.

Perhaps the receptionist thought she was doing her job by overriding a doctor's order that contradicted what she understood to be a policy. Perhaps the receptionist's action was based on her structures of knowing about the organization and her perspective that she was full time and the physician was from an agency and not part of their organization. Whether we are in the right or in the wrong, our decisions and choices are always based on something. If we can understand the basis for our decisions and choices, we can unravel some of the unhealthy patterns that contribute to mismanaged conflict.

The Basis of Choice

Every single choice we make is based on something. A choice can be based on avoiding risk, abiding by a policy, seeking opportunity for the future, having fun in the moment, eliminating boredom, personal growth, or any number of motives. A choice can be a response to what's happened in the past, what's happening in a changing environment, or a choice can be based on what you want to create for the future. Our choices have power if we understand how to use choice in our leadership role.

Let's ask the question: What was the previous example of power and choice based on? Informal power structures, seniority, culture? Maybe the receptionist just thought she could bully a temporary physician. We'll never know for sure, but what we can be sure of is that there was very little consideration of patient well-being where the receptionist was concerned. This physician's experience shows what misalignment looks like when choices are based on something outside of the true mission of the organization.

I've worked with government organizations that struggle with employee motivation and performance, and I can see why. No matter how well an employee performs, there's pressure to give only a 3 out of 5 on the performance evaluation. Frankly, this is unreasonable. This decision is based on ignorance and lack of understanding about how to keep employees engaged. If in the system there's no way to win, why try? The decision to give every performer average scores is based on a justification that there's no budget for raises, or on an assumption that if we give good employees a 5, it doesn't really matter because raises aren't based on performance, only on cost-of-living increases. Choices are always based on something. The question is, Are your choices working for you or against you? *If you don't question your choices, they will become reactive, unconscious, and based on the wrong criteria.*

—— The Distinction between Decision and Choice ——

A lot of confusion could be resolved by making clear distinctions between two words: decision and choice. We often use the words choice and decision interchangeably to mean the same thing, but there's a distinction between decision and choice. A decision is bigger than a choice. A decision is strategic, and a choice is tactical. A decision is the direction—the island, if you will. The choices are the rowers in the boat. Decisions give clarity and direction so that choices are easier to make. That's why they call top leaders "decision-makers." Once a real decision is made, either your choices (smaller decisions) align with that direction or they don't. Nonetheless, a clear decision makes both choosing and course correction easier.

Establishing vision and values is a *decision* that leads to actions (choices) that help to align choices with the decision. Without a decision, our choices can become confusing or inconsistent with what we're trying to achieve. When we base our choices on what other people did, or might do, what might be entertaining, what feels good, what's convenient, or what might hurt someone's feelings, our choices create drama and dysfunction.

—— Action-Decision-Choice Guidelines ——

The following is what I refer to as the action-decision-choice guidelines. These four questions will help you unravel the actions, choices, and decisions of unresolved conflicts where the decisions seem to be incongruent or unequal.

1. Take stock of past activities and actions. Notice if the actions were reactionary or aligned with a bigger decision.

2. When making a choice, think about potential outcomes and consequences of the choice.

3. Examine the basis for your choices. Whether it's a choice you made or one made by an employee, ask the question, "What was this choice based on?"

4. Ask yourself if the power (choice) is equal to the responsibility required. Does the person who made the choice own the responsibility for the result?

Using the example of the receptionist and physician, we can answer all four questions to understand how our decision-making process is working or not working. For the first question, we would say that the receptionist tried to overrule the physician's decision, and most likely this activity would not align with the corporate decision-making process. This either means there's a hands-off leader who doesn't know what's going on or there's some cultural issues that need to be addressed.

For question number two, the consequences of this action would be that the patient may not get the right care, and the physician with years of education and experience would feel undermined and view the receptionist as insubordinate. The crucial impact would be felt years later when patient safety issues came to the surface, patients were lost to other providers, or temporary physicians who found it difficult to work at this location complained.

Using question three, we might say the choice (the receptionist's behavior) was based on ineffective policy or based on a misunderstanding of the decision-making process. This would tell you that the policy needed to be updated or a performance conversation initiated to make sure everyone clearly understood their role and how decisions were made.

To answer question four, the receptionist could not possibly own the patient results—the responsibility belongs to the physician and to the clinic—therefore, the power of choice was out of balance when the receptionist took responsibility for the patient's health decision.

Whoever has the choice is the one who has the responsibility for the consequences of the choice. This requires the choice maker to understand how to align choices with decisions that have already been made. The question we must always be asking is, "Who is responsible?" The answer reveals not the decision but who has the real power of choice.

Signs of Irresponsible Leadership

Employees have responsibility for their work, and the leader has responsibility to ensure that the work is completed. It's much easier to lead (and manage) responsible employees; therefore, everything you do as a leader must be about empowerment instead of enablement.

Yet, sometimes leaders enable employees because they fall into the patterns we talked about in chapter 1: hero, hands-off, or best-friend leaders. The hero or best-friend leaders specifically like to be needed. They overfunction and overcompensate for their employees. They build a community, and they build loyalty, but they often fail to build confidence and competencies. How do you recognize these red flags?

➡ Allowing excuses

➡ Appeasing

➡ Micromanaging

➡ Fixing problems

→ Hiding bigger problems from executives

→ Making promises that aren't kept

→ Missing deadlines

These congenial leaders are easy to get along with, and they are appeasers. They tell employees, vendors, and customers what they want to hear. They also tell their executives "I've got everything handled" and "Things are going well." Their likeability factor is so high that we barely notice that they keep dropping the ball, whether it's paying a bill, being on time to meetings, or following through on deliverables. The very "nice" leaders leave many loose ends, blaming the failures on red tape, regulations, other people, or the workload. You're going to have culture problems if you get a best-friend leader or hero leader who appeases and then breaks promises. Responsibility is the trademark of a good leader who knows how to manage both inner and outer conflict and lives by example. Don't be fooled by congeniality, good personalities, or likeability.

I was working with an executive who was struggling with a VP's performance and felt blindsided when he realized his VP didn't know how to project manage. Instead, the VP saw the tasks as one conglomerate of checklists, and the employees were shooting from the hip on how they processed their work. The priorities were unclear, and there were many mistakes and missed deadlines. As we strategized about the conversation this executive needed to have with this VP, he reported back and told me that the VP made excuses about not having enough time and about feeling misunderstood. In the same breath, he made grandiose promises, which the executive recognized as a past pattern of unmet obligations. At the root, this person doesn't want to disappoint anyone, but they disappoint over and over because of their blind spot of appeasing and avoiding the feeling of having let someone down. While the outer game here might be to learn project management skills, the inner work is learning how to tell an uncomfortable truth about the situation so that the obligations can be fulfilled or expectations can be altered.

The intention is there, but the awareness is not. Excuse making is a sign that a person doesn't recognize choice and therefore spends time reacting instead of preempting.

A sign to look for in those you lead is their ability to see their choices and take ownership for the situation at hand—in other words, their decision-making abilities. Even when resources are low or time runs out, there's the *choice* to keep others in the loop instead of *apologizing after the fact*. A mediocre worker who takes full responsibility and is more conflict capable is a better candidate for leadership than a great technical worker who wants to avoid the heat of responsibility when the going gets tough.

——— Dialing Up Choice and Power ———

Going from worker to leader requires a mindset shift. Many ambitious individuals eagerly seek the leadership title and position without understanding that additional power always equals new responsibilities. Although they were once competent in their former position, their role changes with the promotion. While being a worker meant competing for opportunities, being a leader means collaborating with others.

While being a star employee meant getting the limelight for accomplishments, being a leader means shining the spotlight on others. In your role as a worker, it's admirable to be viewed as a rainmaker or a racehorse; in your role as a leader, your job is to find ways to help others win. In this new role, micromanaging doesn't work. Neither does becoming best friends to avoid confrontation or to avoid the harsh reality of making difficult decisions and having difficult conversations. These unforeseen changes can threaten one's identity momentarily. Leading is never as easy as it looks, and if the new leader won't initiate difficult conversations, they mismanage conflict. The imbalance causes problems later.

The good news is the choice/power factor can be dialed up or down, depending on how much responsibility the employee shows they are capable of. If you currently have leaders who are conflict adverse or who try to be best-friend or hero leaders, it's likely because they were promoted on some qualification that didn't align with the qualities necessary for leadership.

If promotions are given based on seniority or technical skills, the basis of that decision may not produce a great leader. Leadership skills are distinct from the hard skills or technical skills a person performs in their daily role. If it's clear what qualities are needed for leaders in your organization, you can base your decisions on those qualities.

My advice to top leaders is this: Don't dial up power and choice until there's an understanding that more power equals more responsibility. Get clear on what responsibilities, mindsets, and capabilities are needed to lead and manage, and you'll make decisions on who to promote based on values and leadership needs, versus advancing people based on entitlements or seniority.

Going from worker to leader is a difficult shift for most. When you are an employee, it's easy to judge those in leadership positions, but when you become a leader, you realize that there are many lessons to learn. Leadership is as much about the inner game as the outer game of skills. Learning to lead is an ongoing journey that can't be accomplished at a workshop or from watching a few leadership videos. Leadership is a practice based on aligning skills and abilities to values and desired objectives.

Anytime there's a choice, there's an equal requirement of responsibility. Conflict can be a catalyst for change and a chance to grow, or conflict can hamper productivity, inhibit teamwork, affect customer service, and cause irreversible damage. Where there's mismanaged conflict, look for an imbalance between choice and responsibility and look at what new decisions must be made to create balance.

Reflection

1. When have you heard or said "I have no other choice"?

2. How does choice expand power and freedom?

3. What individual in your life do you need to see differently?

4. In what ways do you see people buying into excuses or powerlessness?

It's Worth It

Building courage doesn't happen by taking a course or reading a book; it's a journey. On that journey you'll have to climb Mud Hill. Mud Hill is when you find yourself in resistance, and you don't have the power to shift your energy. Your mud hill might include an employee, a peer, or a boss. Stay the course, even if you still fall into patterns of being too nice or losing your cool. There's time for reflection and course correction. The journey can be arduous, but it's worth your effort.

You'll know it's worth it when you no longer get triggered by the person who used to drive you crazy. You have the ability to interpret the situation differently or the courage to set an appropriate boundary.

It's worth it when you summon the strength to resist winning an argument and, instead, listen radically.

It's worth it when you see improved performance because you initiated a difficult conversation without damaging the relationship.

It's worth it when other people notice that you're different. Instead of criticizing, you're coaching. You have emotional integrity. People trust you. You have influence.

More importantly, it's worth it when you feel the changes within yourself. You hear differently, you see differently, and you speak differently. You listen for narratives that indicate a lack of responsibility. You see choices where others see obstacles. You talk about the future more than about the past. You have the courage to stop avoiding and start leading.

From Conflict to Courage

Study Guide and
Book Club Facilitation

There's nothing like a good conversation to increase awareness and facilitate learning. It's easy to create an intellectually stimulating discussion by hosting a book club. You can host a book club over a period of several weeks, as a half-day session, or with a couple of lunch-and-learn sessions. The first question you need to ask is, Who is the book club for and what is it for?

If your interests are more aligned with personal growth, the questions at the end of each chapter work well.

This facilitation guide offers three questions from each chapter to help you easily facilitate a conversation from the context of the culture and the organization. At the end, you'll find "The Easy Road," a set of questions that don't take a lot of time but still provoke thought.

For more ideas on how to facilitate, or if you are looking for a professional facilitator, email *marlene@marlenechism.com*.

Chapter 1: Conflict Capacity

1. What kind of support could we offer our leaders to expand their conflict capacity?

   a. How would that shape our culture?

   b. What resources do we need to offer this support?

2. What internal factors shape our culture when it comes to leadership effectiveness?

3. What external forces have we experienced that led to increased conflict?

Chapter 2: Identity

1. What is the definition for leadership in your organization?

2. If there isn't a definition, what steps do you need to take to create one?

3. What actions do you see from leaders that indicate they identify with their role?

4. What behaviors do you see the most from new leaders? Hands off, hero, or best friend?

Chapter 3: Leadership Clarity

1. When have you tried to problem-solve before thoroughly understanding the situation?

2. What are the current obstacles and distractions you see leaders facing?

3. Discuss the leadership clarity formula and how you will use it in the future.

Chapter 4: Emotional Integrity

1. Discuss the concept: think of blame as a shortcut for avoiding responsibility. How is accountability different from blame?

2. Where do you see examples of leaders overcompensating instead of coaching?

3. What would improve the way disagreements or complaints are handled?

Chapter 5: Environmental Impact

1. What policies need to be updated to align with the expectations?

2. What would make the work environment more conducive to collaboration?

3. Discuss decision-making as a structure using the Aldi versus Walmart example.

   a. What kind of decisions need to be made to change behaviors with clients?

   b. What kind of decisions need to be made to change behaviors with employees?

   c. Discuss the structures that support employees in your organization.

Chapter 6: Resistance Training

1. What type of conflicts continue to be unresolved due to a lack of willingness?

2. Discuss the three types of resistance:

   a. Your resistance

   b. Their resistance

   c. Your resistance to their resistance

3. How much time or productivity is lost due to resistance?

Chapter 7: Skills

1. Discuss the examples of good intention setting versus poor intention setting.

2. Pick one of the tools in the blueprint and talk about how you plan on using it.

3. Name a past conflict and how this conflict affected the business.

4. Where is the biggest obstacle: clarity, skills, priorities, resources, or willingness?

Chapter 8: Responsibility

1. What red flags indicate a belief that there are "no choices"?

2. Discuss the concept of "growing responsible employees" by helping them recognize choice.

   a. The importance of understanding that their viewpoint may be different from the facts

   b. Helping them see choices they have control over

   c. Not getting distracted by a "victim" narrative

3. Talk about the difference between giving advice and coaching.

   a. How often do leaders blurt out the answer instead of asking questions?

   b. When is it difficult to just listen?

   c. How do you redirect when coaching isn't working?

The Easy Road

These questions are more of a free-for-all discussion meant to generate easy conversation that doesn't take a lot of work. Enjoy!

1. What prompted you to read this book?

2. What concept resonated most with you?

3. What ideas have you tried that worked?

4. What ideas have you tried that felt awkward?

5. What parts of the book didn't apply to you or your current role?

6. Who else needs to read this book?

7. What do you need to do to improve your inner game?

8. Did this book help you see conflict differently? Why or why not?

9. Are there any defining moments you have had due to conflict?

10. Is there a conflict currently unresolved? If so what's your first step?

Notes

Introduction

1 "Workplace Conflict Statistics," Pollack Peacebuilding Systems, *https://pollackpeacebuilding.com/workplace-conflict-statistics/*.

2 "EEOC Releases Fiscal Year 2020 Enforcement and Litigation Data," US Equal Employment Opportunity Commission, February 26, 2021, *https://www.eeoc.gov/newsroom/eeoc-releases-fiscal-year-2020-enforcement-and-litigation-data*.

3 "How Long Does an Employment Discrimination Case Take from Start to Finish," Shegerian & Associates, October 27, 2014, *https://www.shegerianlaw.com/long-employment-discrimination-case-start-finish/*.

Chapter 1

1 Your Dictionary, s.v. "conflict," accessed September 20, 2021, *https://www.yourdictionary.com/conflict*.

Chapter 5

1 Youmi Kim and Mike Ives, "Couple Who Defaced $400,000 Painting Thought It Was a Public Art Project," *New York Times*, April 7, 2021, *https://www.nytimes.com/2021/04/07/world/asia/jonone-vandalism-south-korea-art.html*.

Bibliography

Dispenza, Joe. *Breaking the Habit of Being Yourself: How to Lose Your Mind and Create a New One.* Hay House, 2012.

Drake, David B. *Narrative Coaching: The Definitive Guide to Bringing New Stories to Life.* 2nd ed. CNC Press, 2018.

Dweck, Carol S. *Mindset: The New Psychology of Success.* Random House, 2006.

Fritz, Robert, and Wayne Scott Anderson. *Identity: Why It Doesn't Matter What You Think about Yourself.* Newfane Press, 2016.

Fritz, Robert. *The Path of Least Resistance for Managers.* Berrett-Koehler Publishers, 1999.

Glasser, William. *Choice Theory: A New Psychology of Personal Freedom.* Harper Collins, 1998.

Golas, Thaddeus. *The Lazy Man's Guide to Enlightenment.* The Seed Center, 1973.

Hawkins, David M. *Letting Go: The Pathway of Surrender.* Hay House, 2013.

Hardy, Ben. *Personality Isn't Permanent: Break Free from Self-Limiting Beliefs and Rewrite Your Story.* Portfolio/Penguin, 2020.

Kotler, Steven. *The Art of Impossible: A Peak Performance Primer.* Harper Collins, 2021.

Lerner, Harriet. *The Dance of Anger: A Woman's Guide to Changing the Patterns of Intimate Relationships.* Quill, 2001.

Rock, David. *Your Brain at Work: Strategies for Overcoming Distraction, Regaining Focus, and Working Smarter All Day Long.* Harper Business, 2009.

Scott, Kim. *Radical Candor: Be a Kick-Ass Boss without Losing Your Humanity.* Fully rev. ed. St Martin's Publishing Group, 2019.

Tolle, Eckhart. *The Power of Now: A Guide to Spiritual Enlightenment.* Namaste Publishing, 1999.

Tolle, Eckhart. *A New Earth: Awakening to Your Life's Purpose.* Dutton/Penguin Group, 2005.

Zukav, Gary. *Universal Human.* Simon and Schuster, 2021.

Acknowledgments

I'm honored to be a BK author. I have loved the process from beginning to end. From meeting Neal Maillet, to working with Anna Leinberger on the content, to working with Valerie Caldwell on the cover design. Author's Day, where I met the entire team and presented my vision for this book, was amazing. Inviting my friends and clients to choose the title and allowing me some say in the design was just an added bonus. All of this didn't just happen. Looking back, I see all the relationships and opportunities that led to this book.

First, I'd like to thank Roberta Matuson, who introduced me to LinkedIn Learning, where I've had the privilege of developing several online courses: Anger Management, Difficult Conversations, and Working with High Conflict People as a Manager. It was at LinkedIn Learning where I met Kathe Sweeney, my first content manager. Kathe Sweeney introduced me to Berrett-Koehler as a potential author.

Next, I'd like to thank Cheryl Moreno, former director of Leadership Academy at Express Employment Professionals Headquarters. Cheryl invited me to work with the Leadership Academy to provide executive development for franchise owners on how to have difficult performance conversations. Cheryl has been instrumental in helping me refine the content, test the methods, and measure the results. The blueprint in chapter 7 is possible because of the work I've done with Cheryl and Express Employment Professionals over the last decade. I'm grateful for the successful business owners, the franchisees who have courageously shared their journey and implemented the methods in their own business.

I couldn't do all that I do without my virtual team, who are always responsive and dependable: Kevin Baker, Betty Hardin, Greg Schueler, and Carrie Berkebile. Special thanks to Heather Joyner, who wears many hats and has played many roles, from client to executive assistant, to friend, to certified facilitator.

I appreciate the opportunity to share my ideas and methods about managing conflict. Like many, I've lived the experience where conflict meant a threat to safety and security. I'm grateful for a stable home life where even in conflict, I never doubt my safety and security. I'm thankful to my husband, Gerald, for believing in me and being on the journey with me.

Index

About the Author

MARLENE CHISM works with leaders to build drama-free cultures that drive growth and reduce costly mistakes. Services include consulting, coaching, advisory, executive education, and keynote speaking. Marlene is known for helping managers address "the elephant in the room" and initiate conversations that get results. Her expertise includes leadership development, conflict management, and strategic communication.

Marlene is a recognized expert on the LinkedIn Learning global platform, producing educational videos including Anger Management, Difficult Conversations, Difficult Conversations for Managers, and Working with High Conflict People.

She is the author of *Stop Workplace Drama* (Wiley, 2011), *No-Drama Leadership* (Bibliomotion, 2015), *Stop Drama in Your Healthcare Practice* (Greenbranch, 2018), and *From Conflict to Courage* (Berrett-Koehler, 2022).

Marlene is a seasoned professional speaker, and her transformational message of personal responsibility and alignment is making its way around the globe at leadership academies, corporate retreats, association conferences, and customized webinars.

Marlene has a degree in communications from Drury University and a master's degree in HR development from Webster University. She is an enhanced practitioner of narrative coaching.

To learn more about Marlene, visit *www.marlenechism.com*.

Berrett–Koehler
Publishers

Berrett-Koehler is an independent publisher dedicated to an ambitious mission: *Connecting people and ideas to create a world that works for all.*

Our publications span many formats, including print, digital, audio, and video. We also offer online resources, training, and gatherings. And we will continue expanding our products and services to advance our mission.

We believe that the solutions to the world's problems will come from all of us, working at all levels: in our society, in our organizations, and in our own lives. Our publications and resources offer pathways to creating a more just, equitable, and sustainable society. They help people make their organizations more humane, democratic, diverse, and effective (and we don't think there's any contradiction there). And they guide people in creating positive change in their own lives and aligning their personal practices with their aspirations for a better world.

And we strive to practice what we preach through what we call "The BK Way." At the core of this approach is *stewardship,* a deep sense of responsibility to administer the company for the benefit of all of our stakeholder groups, including authors, customers, employees, investors, service providers, sales partners, and the communities and environment around us. Everything we do is built around stewardship and our other core values of *quality, partnership, inclusion,* and *sustainability.*

This is why Berrett-Koehler is the first book publishing company to be both a B Corporation (a rigorous certification) and a benefit corporation (a for-profit legal status), which together require us to adhere to the highest standards for corporate, social, and environmental performance. And it is why we have instituted many pioneering practices (which you can learn about at www.bkconnection.com), including the Berrett-Koehler Constitution, the Bill of Rights and Responsibilities for BK Authors, and our unique Author Days.

We are grateful to our readers, authors, and other friends who are supporting our mission. We ask you to share with us examples of how BK publications and resources are making a difference in your lives, organizations, and communities at www.bkconnection.com/impact.

Dear reader,

Thank you for picking up this book and welcome to the worldwide BK community! You're joining a special group of people who have come together to create positive change in their lives, organizations, and communities.

What's BK all about?

Our mission is to connect people and ideas to create a world that works for all.

Why? Our communities, organizations, and lives get bogged down by old paradigms of self-interest, exclusion, hierarchy, and privilege. But we believe that can change. That's why we seek the leading experts on these challenges—and share their actionable ideas with you.

A welcome gift

To help you get started, we'd like to offer you a **free copy** of one of our bestselling ebooks:

www.bkconnection.com/welcome

When you claim your **free ebook**, you'll also be subscribed to our blog.

Our freshest insights

Access the best new tools and ideas for leaders at all levels on our blog at ideas.bkconnection.com.

Sincerely,

Your friends at Berrett-Koehler